Transformative Digital Technology for Effective Workplace Learning

T0383668

Transformative Digital Technology for Effective Workplace Learning

Ria O'Donnell

CRC Press
Taylor & Francis Group
Boca Raton London New York

CRC Press is an imprint of the
Taylor & Francis Group, an **informa** business

AN AUERBACH BOOK

First edition published [2022]
by CRC Press

6000 Broken Sound Parkway NW, Suite 300, Boca Raton, FL 33487-2742

and by CRC Press
4 Park Square, Milton Park, Abingdon, Oxon, OX14 4RN

CRC Press is an imprint of Taylor & Francis Group, LLC

ISBN: 978-1-032-14632-4 (hbk)
ISBN: 978-0-367-71062-0 (pbk)
ISBN: 978-1-003-14913-2 (ebk)

DOI: 10.1201/9781003149132

Typeset in Garamond
by SPi Technologies India Pvt Ltd (Straive)

For my loving husband Sean, who patiently supported every single moment of the writing journey.

Contents

Preface

As a lifelong educator and writer, I've planned to write several books on learning, and this is hopefully the first of many. Education and writing are two of the great passions of my life. Education because it is the enabler of improvement, growth, and success, and writing because it is an enduring form of communication that allows the reader to work systematically through ideas, concepts, and solutions with clarity and purpose.

With an early career as a school teacher and a teacher-librarian, the focus on emerging digital technologies intrigued me. I was always at the forefront of advancements in the learning space, experimenting with ideas and discovering exciting solutions to educational problems. It wasn't until I moved into the corporate sector as a learning and development practitioner that comparisons were drawn between learning in the classroom and learning in the workplace. For the most part, learning in the workplace seemed to garner far less interest and investment and was treated as an 'optional extra,' far underutilizing its potential.

'Lifelong learning' and 'learning in the workplace,' in my opinion, are simply not valued as they should be. This astounded me, as the benefits of education had always been at the forefront of my work and studies. I realized that the overall profile of learning and development needs to be elevated significantly. Therefore, I endeavored to research the reasons behind this, along with the opportunities for its advancement.

The decision to focus on digital technologies to facilitate this was an easy decision as our lives are entrenched in technology, particularly in the workplace. These technologies don't only improve the ways we work but also greatly improve overall learning experiences. The design, development, delivery, and measurement of learning outcomes in the workplace are enhanced by exciting technologies such as virtual reality, artificial intelligence, and learning analytics.

Having completed a Master of Education with a focus on teacher-librarianship over a decade ago, I decided to return to university and complete a second Master of Education degree, this time focusing on the topics of policy and globalization. As part of these studies, I was lucky enough to participate in a study trip to Singapore. During that time, I witnessed the Singapore Government's incredible dedication to lifelong learning and education at all levels, facilitated by digital technologies. In my view, this formed a benchmark for how everyone should be continuously learning throughout their careers and how it is in contrast to the way many company's currently operate – essentially neglecting ongoing education.

Further to this, I gained an improved understanding of the contributing factors that have changed the nature of learning in the workplace such as globalization and the gig-economy among other things that will be discussed in this book. It became evident that workplace learning and lifelong learning, in general, need to be seriously re-examined for the betterment of all businesses and all individuals. Unfortunately, this area is not only undervalued, but it is under-researched and under-developed in relation to the opportunities it can promise.

Furthermore, as the year 2020 came around and the COVID-19 pandemic arrived uninvitedly, it cemented the necessity for continuous learning and accelerated the need for business leaders and individuals to change their attitudes and approaches to education and technology.

My motivation for publishing this book is to see workplace learning transformed and becoming a central part of every business strategy and every individual's continuous quest for personal and professional development.

Hopefully, what you'll get from this book is a new perspective on what lifelong learning has to offer, how it can transform yourself and your business, and the practical implications of technology-enhanced learning in the workplace today.

Author

Ria O'Donnell is a training consultant with decades of experience in advanced learning technologies. She holds a Master of Education degree which focuses on technology and a Graduate Certificate in Education focusing on globalization. Ria spent her early career as a classroom teacher before moving into learning and development in the corporate sector where she now enables businesses to succeed through effective training programs.

Introduction

We have no idea what the workplace will look like in 2050. Digital technologies are likely to impact almost every line of work, every business, and every industry worldwide. What we do know, however, is that the only thing certain is continuous transformation and that in order to stay properly informed, sustainable, and relevant, whether you are a business or an individual, we need to raise the profile of lifelong learning and the adoption of workplace learning in general.

In a world bursting with new information, ideas, opportunities, and technological advancements, it is time to rethink how continuous learning shapes our future. Amidst the ongoing digital revolution, widespread educational reform, and the most significant global pandemic of our lifetimes, we are at a pivotal time in history.

This book explores the technological developments that are rapidly unfolding in the workplace and those that support workplace training. What emerges is that the rate of change and the possibilities for improvement are more extensive than many of us might have suspected. From artificial intelligence to virtual reality, from data analytics to adaptive learning, there is the capacity for significant innovation and opportunity if harnessed in the right ways.

The goal of this book is not to merely describe technological advancements in the workplace but instead, to challenge the status quo and think critically about the future that lies ahead. The aim is to have business leaders understand the necessity for ongoing workplace learning and also have the individual appreciate that lifelong learning is the new social norm. Ongoing education allows people to become more open to change and less anxious about new experiences.

DOI: 10.1201/9781003149132-1

Developing a growth mindset and adopting a company culture that says everyone can learn new things and continue to improve their performance will become the standard. Most importantly, as the business world is reconfigured before our very eyes, ongoing learning must become an economic imperative.

The topics covered in this book are by no means exhaustive. Instead, it offers an overview of several critical issues that face the future of the workplace and examines them through the lens of lifelong learning. The book begins by conveying the current impacts on the workplace and how the internal function of learning and development has evolved. We then consider the eight learning imperatives that drive workplace learning in this current, volatile state we live in. After which, we examine three predictions of how the future workplace may be resembled. The next section of the book explores technological frameworks for digitally enhanced workplace learning and takes a deeper dive into two particular areas of interest: (1) the capabilities of immersive technologies and (2) the insights enabled through learning analytics that can drive improved business outcomes. Finally, there is an evaluation of future digital trends in the workplace, before offering inspiration to entrepreneurs interested in leveraging the significant opportunities that lay before us.

Following is a brief description of each chapter.

Technology and the New Normal

Today's world has put increasing pressure on businesses and individuals via external impacts such as globalization, the digital revolution, and, more recently, the COVID-19 pandemic. Organizations across the globe experienced significant changes that are redefining many of the characteristics of business operations. In response to these changes, many companies are evaluating and investing in the development, knowledge, and skills of their workforce. Chapter 1 examines how this response will improve the outlook for businesses and lead to empowered workers who can optimize their talents on a continuous trajectory.

As we live through a time of the most rapid changes in history and have recently been thrust into a further acceleration of change, the ability to innovate, adapt, and learn has never been more critical. Change is upon us, and the new normal has become, if it wasn't already, fluid.

It's easy to write about such ongoing change as if employers and workers everywhere will adapt, but this is far from the case. Transformation is complex, and it takes strong leaders and visions to get it right. Change is constant, and everyone and everything is undergoing continual change throughout their lives. Therefore, if you aren't aware of how to develop your path to lifelong learning and make the decisions around the future of your employment or your workplace, the decisions will be made for you. These changes are much more challenging to navigate.

The opportunities that digital technologies afford to enhance workplace learning should not be understated. Digital technologies don't only provide the tools for learning, but in many cases, they dictate what should be learned. By leveraging these technologies, rather than working against them, we can gain the best of what is on offer.

Learning and Development: Evolution and Impacts

Chapter 2 contemplates our improved technology landscape and asks to what extent we can enhance opportunities to integrate education into daily life. By challenging assumptions and reassessing our ideas through continuous development and improvement, we can begin to adjust to more sustainable ways of working in the future. In light of recent threats to the workplace (i.e., the COVID-19 pandemic), and threats to our jobs (i.e., robotics and automation), there are simple shifts in mindset that can occur to improve the outlook for both.

Organizational transformations are occurring due to several factors, resulting in steep learning curves for most of the workforce. While the future for the learning and development function in the workplace holds exciting prospects, there are also many challenges to overcome. There is a bias in the nature of education that, until recent times, tilted it toward school, college, and university, and leaned away from continuous, lifelong learning. This stems from the notion that knowledge is conclusive and limited, an idea that is clearly and significantly outdated.

This section will lead you to a deeper understanding of technology's untapped potential in education and training and how organizations might adopt it. The possibilities are becoming limitless, and learners themselves are becoming empowered to choose their own pathways.

Eight Learning Imperatives

The roll-out of digital learning programs requires thoughtful consideration to upskill and reskill and also embeds a culture of lifelong and continuous learning. Eight learning imperatives should underpin these programs, making them practical and sustainable as we move into the future. These eight learning imperatives are adaptability, engagement, flexibility, personalization, accessibility, social learning, meaningful assessment, and relevance, and can be considered the foundation for modern learning design.

Adaptability looks at adaptable skills, mindsets, and learning resources and how these can provide core competencies and transferable skillsets to individuals. *Engagement* considers the individual, the task, and the environment through which the worker learns and operates. *Flexibility* endeavors to create suitable experiences for all individuals and examine common methods such as the flipped classroom and microlearning. *Personalization* is the approach that aims to customize learning to the individual's unique requirements.

The next learning imperative is *accessibility*, which considers how barriers to learning can be reduced or removed wherever possible. *Social learning* is the idea that groups can share, enhance and encourage ongoing learning experiences. *Meaningful assessment* and the ways its resulting data can be utilized is the next imperative to consider, and finally, *relevance* aims to ensure learning programs align with company strategy while being targeted to the needs of the worker.

Throughout the second chapter, these learning imperatives are explored through the viewpoint of technological advancement and the future of workplace learning and can be used in conjunction with or as the basis of an ongoing learning design framework.

The Digital Future of the Workplace: Three Possible Scenarios

The digital revolution has forced a paradigm shift that will change how organizations operate forever. Chapter 4 considers three possible scenarios for the future and how technological advancements can assist with workplace learning within each predicted model. The three predicted scenarios are identified as (1) the human-centered design approach, (2) integrated artificial intelligence, and (3) the agile adaptors. While each of these predicted possibilities has distinct characteristics, the most likely future scenario will assimilate features of all three projections to varying degrees.

The future of business can no longer be predicted by extrapolating present situations to define future possibilities, as these alternatives are too complex, ambiguous, and infinite. The state of constant flux in the future workplace means we need more than just distinct predictions and leads to the realization that processes now become more important than products. It's about the means rather than the end.

As we find ourselves on the path to whatever future workplace scenario unfolds, both individuals and businesses can fail if we are not prepared. Established organizations can collapse because their business models are no longer relevant, and entire occupations will disappear as new occupations are born. It could be said that those who are ready to embrace the ongoing nature of learning are most likely to succeed.

Technological Frameworks for Success

As advancements in technology-aided learning provide opportunities that were previously unavailable to many, it is becoming more commonplace for organizations to implement frameworks that can enable such learning. Without the ability to foresee what the future holds, a sound technological framework provides the foundations to support organizations and their workers' ever-changing requirements.

Three frameworks have been examined in Chapter 5, which are the Learning Ecosystem Framework 2.0, the Technology Enhanced Learning Framework, and the Digital Workplace Skills Framework. These models were selected for their relevance to the workplace of the future, and we consider that their implementation can secure the most appropriate infrastructure, resources, policies, and programs for successful workplace learning.

For companies who realize that continuous learning should form part of the core of their business strategy, the investment in proper technological frameworks to support workplace learning is essential. These frameworks provide the tools required and aid in governance, maintenance, standards, and internal buy-in for ongoing learning programs.

Learning Analytics: Paving the Way to Improved Educational Outcomes

Chapter 6 discusses the progress and potential of learning analytics in the workplace and the trends that influence its advancement. Because learning analytics provides insights that can lead to effective learning design, it is relevant to consider how to best capture this data. Several strategies can help organizations get started with learning analytics, including defining objectives, adopting agreed-upon standards such as the xAPI specifications, and linking data from multiple sources to monitor, measure, and manage information.

Learning analytics has been adopted far more widely in schools and universities than within the workplace, which again highlights the need to raise the profile of workplace learning to be included as a serious staple of organizational design. However, as the use of data analytics, in general, is realized in the workplace, there is an opportunity for growth and adaptation. Just as data about customers is the new gold for marketing and sales, data about workplace learning is the new gold for continuous development.

Immersive Technologies for Workplace Learning

Immersive educational technologies, most commonly recognized as virtual reality and augmented reality, have gained significant attention because of their ability to bring the user into a sensory environment. Implicit to immersive technologies is the fact that the user must be actively engaged in what they are learning, and the participants generally tend to be more motivated to learn.

Chapter 7 outlines some of the benefits and challenges of using these technologies to support workplace learning. Shorter time to mastery, reduced risks, and improved memory retention are among the benefits. However, these benefits are offset by the cost of setup, limited flexibility, and mixed user experiences. While there is progress still to be made in terms of widespread adoption and seamless experiences, the use of virtual reality and augmented reality is growing, nevertheless.

An area with huge potential to rapidly expand and develop, immersive technologies take traditional learning and morph it into something different entirely. We examine the impact of these technologies on workplace learning and conclude that they should undoubtedly have a place in workplace learning in the future.

Emerging Trends for Digital Workplace Learning

Emerging technologies reimagine the way workplace learning can be designed and delivered. Chapter 8 is divided into two sections. The first examines some of the driving forces behind technological trends for learning, including changes in workforce composition, the shifting learning landscape, the digital economy, newly defined workplace roles, investment in technology, and the workforce's disruption and decentralization. Understanding what is driving such innovation contributes significantly toward optimizing what the resulting digital technologies have to offer.

The second section considers the digital trends themselves and their capacity to make significant impacts on workplace learning. These trends include artificial intelligence, personalized learning, comprehensive learner records, mobile learning, microlearning, and learning experience platforms. Each of these offers unique enhancements to learning in the workplace.

These evolving tools provide the ability to access, share, assess, personalize, and collaborate in ways that are more effective and easier than ever before. The digital age is revolutionizing the way people learn, and by understanding and embracing this, we can tap into opportunities we previously thought inconceivable.

EdTech for the Modern Start-Up

In the final chapter, we take a different approach to technology-enhanced learning. Here, we discuss the creation of innovative technologies and consider the current landscape of EdTech for the aspiring entrepreneur. As the demand for educational technologies increases and deepens, there are market opportunities ready to be filled. The probability that online education will continue to expand exponentially across the globe is very high, and as a result, investors are showing increasing interest.

Creatively designed EdTech solutions can address significant problems facing education around the globe. This chapter deviates from the focus on workplace learning and considers the entire education spectrum from early childhood to adult education. We examine some popular EdTech technologies, including mobile applications, immersive technologies, learning analytics, artificial intelligence, and gamification, while also encouraging further expansion into new technological spheres. The digital revolution has a firm grip on the world, and it is time for creative entrepreneurs to harness the tools we have at our disposal to craft new and exciting ways of engaging learners across the globe, ultimately improving educational outcomes for all.

Collectively, these nine chapters aim to inform and inspire continuous learning as a standard and expected way of life. The content of this book aspires to spark critical thinking and challenge previously held assumptions about the nature of lifelong learning and the digital technologies that might enable it.

Information is no longer limited, skillsets are no longer static, and knowledge is no longer conclusive. These outdated ideas, which are embedded in the minds of many, must be challenged for us to thrive in the modern workplace. From a financial perspective, an organization that invests in developing its workforce continuously will acquire highly valuable human assets, multiplying the return on investment. From a personal point of view, workers will be empowered to direct their professional pathways, be active participants in their development, and even improve the quality of life.

Chapter 1

Technology and the New Normal

Several external influences have impacted workplace learning over recent years. While some of these impacts have been unfolding over time, we are now at a tipping point where the convergence of multiple, significant influences has forced the nature of work to change. In turn, this obliges us to reevaluate how people learn.

Prior to the COVID-19 pandemic, many leaders worldwide believed that the digital revolution was the most intense impact the workplace had ever seen, and while this is in many ways true, the global pandemic has further accelerated the digital influence. As a result, workplace learning has transformed from being occasional, formal, and static to being an ongoing expectation for all workers as learning becomes recognized as a crucial part of working life. In this chapter, we examine the external influences on workplace learning, such as the impacts of technology, globalization, the COVID-19 pandemic, the gig economy, and the rise of robotics. We then look at the internal influences, including remote work practices and the underpinning learning culture within an organization. Finally, we consider the necessity for lifelong learning so that everyone has the opportunity to adapt and excel throughout times of change.

DOI: 10.1201/9781003149132-2

External Influences

External influences, circumstances, and situations are outside of a company's control. There are many external factors influencing business today, some of them are the most significant of our lifetimes. While companies cannot control these external impacts, they need to effectively manage them so they can achieve their strategic objectives. All of these external impacts significantly affect learning within an organization.

The Impact of Technology

Digital technologies within the workplace have undeniably changed the way we operate and interact. The advancement of digital tools has increased flexibility, improved access to training on an ongoing basis, and delivered enhanced solutions in almost every workplace area. From the early 2000s, the trends driving the digital workplace began changing our lives significantly and have been evolving ever since. From the widespread adoption of internet connectivity and email, which then extended to smartphones, SaaS, and the cloud, and more recently to virtual reality, artificial intelligence, and big data, processes have evolved and improved exponentially (Shivakumar, 2020) (Figure 1.1).

New skills are required to operate these evolving technologies, and this requires training on an ongoing basis. The nature of most technologies is that they are continuously enhanced and updated

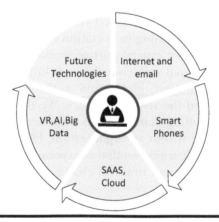

Figure 1.1 Trends driving the digital workplace.

(Shivakumar, 2020), and the associated new knowledge needs to be transferred as updates occur. Learning how to work with new technologies is an ongoing process as we progress into using more and more advanced tools. Though this does not mean that the digital tools become more challenging to use, it just means that the acquisition of the skills and knowledge required to use them is incremental and often builds upon previously mastered skillsets.

Technological advancements inside and outside of the workplace also impact workers in terms of automation and other enhancements that can replicate the tasks that the worker performs. From this view, eliminating some jobs (or parts of some jobs) is a reality that cannot be ignored. While, in many cases, automation certainly has its benefits and is worthy of adoption and further development, at the same time, many people are justifiably concerned about their employment prospects as a result (Harari, 2019; Nguyen, 2020). Regardless of whether there are mass job losses or not, we can safely assume that there will be significant needs for further education. As new technologies such as artificial intelligence are rolled out across businesses, they will not be implemented in a single event, after which workplaces would settle into a new equilibrium (Harari, 2019). Instead, incremental changes will occur over time, with varying impact and complexity, and with each step, there will be various requirements for training and adaptation.

However, while technology may be one of the reasons that continuous training is required, it can also serve as the enabler of the training (Figure 1.2).

Learning technologies have progressed significantly over recent years and continue to provide innovative solutions that allow

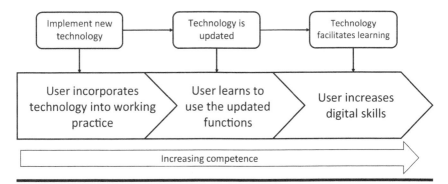

Figure 1.2 Technology-driven training.

workplace learning to become mobile, personalized, flexible, and accessible. Technology brings advantages to workplace learning with the ability to save time, money, and travel, and it also helps to overcome the difficulties associated with scheduling (Short & Greener, 2014). More importantly, it brings opportunities for engagement and immersion through targeted content and rich analytics that provide essential insights to drive learning design.

Digital technologies have also begun to break down the barriers of distance, time, and accessibility for many workers by enabling instant access to their virtual workspaces. With laptops, cloud applications, smartphones, and social platforms, workers can tap into their colleagues, programs, and files without attending a physical office. The virtual office had been steadily paving its way through the 21st century with the popularization of offshore contracting and outsourcing (Nath, Sridhar, Adya, & Malik, 2010; Ramalingam & Mahalingam, 2011) and was then thrust into widespread adoption across the world as a result of the recent global pandemic. Since being forced out of our old ways of working and experiencing a new locked-down and travel-banned reality, the future of workplace technology and workplace learning is only just becoming realized.

Overall, technology is a vast, overarching factor that determines much of how we work and learn. It opens new possibilities and leads to an ongoing requirement for education while at the same time offering enhanced tools that enable the respective learning.

Globalization

Globalization is defined by Merriam-Webster (2021) as "*the development of an increasingly integrated global economy marked especially by free trade, free flow of capital, and the tapping of cheaper foreign labor markets.*" It is significantly impacting how we work and interact, and most importantly, how we acquire new knowledge. An expanded depiction of globalization, relevant to this topic, comes from Arnold (2020), who describes a multifaceted phenomenon that is progressive, democratic, and modernizing, while at the same time complex, volatile, economically efficient, and technologically sophisticated (Figure 1.3).

There are impacts to the ways of working as a result of greater competition, increased outsourcing, increased technology, policy updates, cultural diversity, and the complex and volatile nature of the workplace as a result. All of these things require the workforce

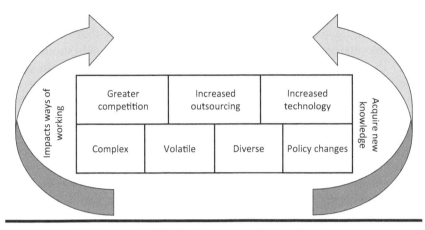

Figure 1.3   The impact of globalization on workplace learning.

to acquire new knowledge. Consequently, Arnold (2020) says that there are inevitable negative drawbacks, including job losses, standardization of goods and services, protectionism, over-consumption, and business relocations.

On all accounts, the world seems to be getting smaller as interconnectivity unites people, companies, and cultures across space and time; however, globalization brings opportunities and constraints to workplace learning. Opportunities may come in the form of innovation, increased access to people and resources, a more extensive knowledge bank, a more diverse range of digital solutions, and often the reduced price of content and associated technologies. In comparison, constraints may include lack of stability and direction due to the myriad of perspectives, the overwhelming array of information and content to choose from, and in some cases, cybersecurity weaknesses and difficulty in validating authentic programs. This means that knowledge is regularly evaluated, revised, and updated, and as a result, it is expected that learning should be continuous in nature to reflect this.

In addition to these opportunities and constraints, there are other considerations to be made, such as the impact of cultural diversity. Globalization increases cultural diversity both within the workplace and outside of the workplace when interacting with external contractors, business partners, and clients. Cultural differences can present in many ways within the workplace, ranging from values and assumptions to tacit knowledge that cannot be easily transferred (Ramalingam & Mahalingam, 2011). Because cultural values govern an individual's behavior, they can extensively influence how learning takes place, as well as the context of the knowledge that is absorbed (Rensink, 2016). Learning and development professionals should consider the ongoing education required around how people can work effectively with others who may have different customs, etiquette, and world views. Moreover, when designing training programs, they should also consider that different people may have very different styles of learning and contextualizing information (Joy & Kolb, 2009). Thus training opportunities should be meaningful, considerate, accessible, and relevant to its target audience.

Consequently, globalization has a substantial impact on how work is evolving and the ideas and knowledge that should be transferred among various groups of people. Interconnectivity is intensifying, information is increasing, and innovation is driving continuous updates to skills and knowledge. Therefore, lifelong learning is imperative as we each navigate our unique pathways of professional and personal development.

COVID-19 Pandemic

One of the most significant global impacts of our lifetime was the COVID-19 pandemic. Periods of lockdown, social distancing, and the pivoting of business operations extensively changed how we work and learn forever. Many standard practices suddenly became obsolete, and the global fallout served as the ultimate disruptor, forcing innovation and new ways of thinking to the forefront (Bennett & McWhorter, 2021).

There was also a significant impact on individual workers. Many people were pushed out of employment or into under-employment or unstable jobs. This called for them to rethink their learning paths and pave a new way for work in the future. For many, this is a more difficult task than it may seem, as, particularly for older generations, the attitude and ability for lifelong learning had not previously been understood (Donorfio & Chapman, 2020). During the pandemic, the need for upskilling, reskilling, learning, and unlearning was immediate, and many people were not equipped to manage this successfully. It would be optimistic to think that lifelong learning will be globally addressed as we move into the future, so should crisis strike again, it would enable the workforce at large to be better prepared.

Nevertheless, as a result of the general disruption, the shifts in technology were rapid and, in many cases, experimental. As outlined in the McKinsey Global Survey (2020), many organizations undertook several years' worth of technological development within a few short months, making workplace learning a higher priority than ever before. Workers needed to learn how to use new technologies and master new skills as they transitioned through changes (Bennett & McWhorter, 2021). The COVID-19 pandemic has undoubtedly accelerated the shift toward virtual learning, and most workplaces now realize that, at least as a contingency plan, their training programs need the ability to be delivered online.

The COVID-19 pandemic also brought about the requirement of a new series of training programs to be introduced into various organizations. Many learning and development specialists redeveloped training programs to incorporate the following:

1. COVID-safe procedures for the workplace to ensure the safety of customers and workers.
2. Digital literacy training to enable workers to continue activities from their 'virtual workspace.'
3. Upskilling staff on how to perform functions that have been altered or updated.
4. Reskilling staff to enable them to perform new roles if the company's products or service offerings have changed.
5. Soft-skill training to enable workers to effectively communicate and collaborate using new 'virtual' methods and protocols.
6. Training on new legal or compliance implications that have been imposed on the business due to the pandemic.
7. Ongoing learning experiences focusing on innovation and problem-solving skills that can assist businesses in their recovery (Figure 1.4).

It becomes evident that learning and development in the workplace must become an elevated function for businesses to prosper in the post-pandemic era (Bennett & McWhorter, 2021). The above learning programs are expected now and into the future and form a part of foundational training in many workplaces. Education has been necessary to enable remote working, and at the same time, training has become virtual, leading to a steeper but necessary learning curve. Many of the changes brought about by the pandemic are here to stay, and many will generate further developments and innovative advances once we settle into the new normal.

Figure 1.4   Impacts of COVID-19 on workplace training programs.

The Gig Economy

As defined by the Oxford Dictionary (2021), the gig economy is *"a labor market characterized by the prevalence of short-term contracts or freelance work as opposed to permanent jobs."* It is named after the slang word for a job that lasts for a short, specified period, traditionally used in the music industry. These short-term 'gigs' are typical in occupations such as driving, delivery, consulting, design, and software development. For this discussion, the gig economy will be split into two defined groups. The first, being the more controversial group of wealthy, international companies such as Uber and Deliveroo, that pay individuals per 'job' completed, though they do not employ the worker, meaning that the worker receives no standard employment benefits such as overtime, paid leave or compensation if they have an accident (Vallas & Schor, 2020). The second group comprises workers who engage in short-term projects, often through companies such as Upwork or Fiverr, which may take anywhere from several hours to several months to complete. These workers are also not employed and receive very limited contractual benefits, though the structure allows workers to set their pay and progress rates as they gain a positive reputation (Vallas & Schor, 2020). It is this second group that is referred to in this section.

The trend toward the gig economy has gathered speed over the past decade and has more recently seen a sharp acceleration due to the impacts of the COVID-19 pandemic. As many workers were pushed out of their usual jobs or had their hours reduced, they switched to freelance-style employment. Some people have moved to this type of work full-time, while others can complete projects in their free time, outside of their primary employment (Stephany, Dunn, Sawyer, & Lehdonvirta, 2020).

The impact on workplace learning is evident as employees learn to manage relationships with external providers and the ongoing changes that occur as the number of contracted workers scale up and down according to the company's requirements (Stephany et al., 2020). However, the more significant impact is on the freelancers themselves as they adapt to working with a variety of companies, self-managing their employment, and keeping their skills current. For these professionals, lifelong learning is an essential characteristic that will allow them to sustain work in the gig economy. There is also a third impact on workplace learning which has been underexplored, which is training for all parties involved around legal obligations, insurance contracts, tax responsibilities, and the contractual obligations to the technology platforms that connect the worker to the client (Stephany et al., 2020; Vallas & Schor, 2020) (Figure 1.5).

Overall, the gig economy is a controversial but growing method of working around the world. It has significant benefits and risks that may offset one another in various ways depending on each individual's unique situation. However, so long as it is regulated responsibly, it will continue to influence working practices and the consequential training requirements within the workplace.

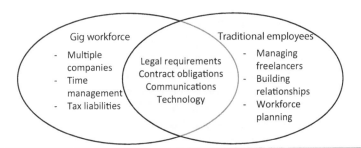

Figure 1.5 Impacts of the gig economy on various types of workers.

Robotics and Automation

Robotics, which can be described as *"a field of research that includes computer science, mechanical and electronics engineering, and science process intending to produce robots, or related forms of automation, to replicate human tasks"* (Barbara et al., 2018), is another controversial topic when it comes to the future of work and learning. While there are infinite possibilities for what robotics, automation, and other forms of artificial intelligence can do for workplace operations, there is also the justifiable concern that it may threaten many jobs. A McKinsey Global Institute study of 800 occupations across almost 50 countries revealed that around 20% of the global workforce (or 800 million jobs) could be replaced by robotics by 2030 (Barbara et al., 2018).

However, this is not to say that these workers will be displaced, though if their jobs are affected in part or in full, there will be a fundamental requirement for widespread reskilling. There should always be new opportunities for work that have not yet been contemplated, and should workers' time be freed up due to the gradual implementation of robotic automation, then new employment ideas could be given further consideration. Instead of competing with robotic automation, humans should focus instead on servicing and leveraging their capabilities (Harari, 2019).

A reassuring narrative by Kelly (2017) suggests that one skill that humans possess that robots do not is the ability to decide what robots should be programmed to do. Two hundred years ago, industrialization enabled part of the population to discover that there were more things for humans to do than strive to feed and clothe themselves. They discovered they could spend their lives as musicians, athletes, novelists, fashion designers, and other occupations that they would not have been afforded if their time was spent ensuring their basic survival. In the same way, in the future, there will be more discoveries that can fill humans' time and attention and provide an income if robots complete the work that these people previously undertook. In other words, it is not a race against the robots; it is a race with the robots. If we race against them, we are likely to lose, though if we race alongside them, leveraging the opportunities they bring, there will be far more significant possibilities for all (Kelly, 2017).

There are, however, many societies that are actively embracing the use of robotics. In Japan's cultural opinion, robots are not considered threats but rather solutions to many critical problems (Barbara et al., 2018), such as performing rote functions unappealing to the average worker, disassembling bombs and delivering services in dangerous or remote environments. The organizations and individuals who embrace robotic technologies and leverage the opportunities they bring will need to shift their focus to educating themselves on managing and maintaining their robots, programming them to improve, and operating robotic technologies across the workplace. These skills may become the new norm, while at the same time if workers are educated in higher-level thinking skills such as creativity and problem solving, they will be more likely to bring new and innovative solutions to the business. Either way, whether robotics enable workers or threaten their livelihoods, there is a clear call for lifelong learning to be at the forefront of all workers' agendas who want to thrive in the future.

Internal Influences

In addition to several significant external influences, there are also internal impacts within organizations that affect how working and learning will progress into the future. The two most noteworthy developments are the trend toward remote working and the internal culture of learning within the workplace.

Remote Working

The acceptance of the virtual workspace has contributed to the more widespread popularity of flexible working arrangements. These working arrangements may include features such as the ability to work partially or entirely from home (or another location), job sharing, flexi-time, and the compressed workweek (working longer hours over fewer days).

Because flexible working arrangements are becoming increasingly accepted, and many workplaces now comprise at least some staff working remotely (Nath et al., 2010), workers need to be educated on managing this. Remote working is a significant internal impact on workplace learning for several reasons. The most notable is that workers need to learn how to best use the technology that enables virtual working and adapt to new structures such as digital communication protocols. Both onsite and remote workers need to learn the skills required to communicate successfully, collaborate across distances, and respect one another's working situations. It also brings digital skills into focus, as technological advancements enable such working arrangements. Knowing how to utilize the available digital tools is increasingly essential, as is the development of soft skills

(Bennett & McWhorter, 2021) as workers expand their interactions with people from various demographics.

Learning and development professionals are creating online opportunities that can be delivered asynchronously and from various devices. This type of learning is becoming the new normal and allows for workers' consistent opportunity regardless of their geographical working arrangements. While there will be many post-pandemic studies to come in the future, there are currently contradicting findings around remote working that reveal positive and negative impacts for workers and businesses. Studies carried out by Dilmaghani (2020) found that employees with flexible working arrangements reported significantly higher job satisfaction. In addition to this, other studies show that when employers permit such flexibility, the employee often feels compelled to reciprocate by showing greater commitment and job involvement (Casper & Buffardi, 2004), leading to improved outcomes for both parties. On the other hand, there can also be negative consequences such as feelings of isolation for those working remotely and the view that if they are not visible to management, then it reduces their prospects of career advancement and other opportunities (Dilmaghani, 2020). These things will be considered as many organizations settle into new normal ways of flexible working (Bennett & McWhorter, 2021). While many companies and managers may resist this way of working, many also embrace it, and it is clear that remote working is here to stay, at least in some capacity.

However, regardless of where, when, and how people work, it is encouraging to see that a rising number of businesses recognize that the delivery of outcomes is what should actually be measured. The delivery of outcomes is increasingly perceived as being a more meaningful contribution than the number of supervised hours an employee spends in the physical workplace.

Learning Culture

A learning culture is the expression of an organization's conventions, values, practices, and processes that encourage the creation and sharing of knowledge (Richardson & Richardson, 2017). Organizations with positive learning cultures can provide and encourage opportunities that elevate individuals both professionally and personally and improve business outcomes as a result.

As organizations are becoming increasingly aware that ongoing learning is required to remain competitive in the future marketplace, attract the best talent, and improve their business offerings, an increasing number of companies are planning for such transition (Bennett & McWhorter, 2021). A company's learning culture is somewhat of a silent, internal impact. As whether it is positive or negative, strong or weak, or somewhere in between, it is significantly impacting many aspects of how the company operates. According to Totterdill (2013), several essential qualities are observable in a positive learning organization. These include employee engagement, a proper technology framework, autonomy for individuals and teams, trust of colleagues and respect for the organization, and finally, a positive workspace that brings these things together.

The benefits of a learning organization have been widely recognized since the 1980s, though the serious commitment to this concept has been relatively slow and staggered (Totterdill, 2013). Learning organizations take pride in documenting their knowledge as it is acquired and keeping it up to date. They also see value in documenting experiments and failures (Totterdill, 2013), as this forms part of the learning curve and provides reference material for employees who wish to reengage with such problems at a later time. Knowledge is cataloged, and more importantly, shared throughout the organization. All workers should have access to knowledge repositories, and all workers feel they can make a valuable contribution (Richardson & Richardson, 2017).

Despite the well-researched and documented benefits of a positive learning culture in the workplace, McKinsey and Company (Grossman, 2015) found that only ten percent of companies have proper learning cultures. However, it is reasonably safe to assume that this number will significantly increase if the newfound global recognition that a positive learning culture is required, matches subsequent implementations.

Overall, the health of an organization's learning culture has a substantial impact on the workers' performance, how they work together and how they incrementally progress. In turn, this has considerable effects on the direction and performance of the entire organization.

The Necessity for Lifelong Learning

In 2021, the question is no longer 'do we need to engage in lifelong learning?' but instead 'how do we enable lifelong learning for everyone?' This question is imperative for every business and every individual who wants to excel in the post-pandemic future.

Lifelong learning is a term that has been around for decades and is increasing in popularity. The European Commission (2001) defines it as *"all learning activity undertaken throughout life, with the aim of improving knowledge, skills and competencies within a personal, civic, social and/or employment-related perspective."* While there are many definitions on offer depending on the context for which they are used, the basic principle is that it is no longer feasible to expect that the knowledge and skills acquired during school, college, and university will equip people to prosper throughout their lifetime (London, 2011). Instead, we need to keep the pace with the developments in information, knowledge, and technologies that underpin the learning that will keep us evolving.

In the 21st century, knowledge and skills need to be continually revised and updated due to new discoveries, understandings, and methods that reflect the reality of continuous change. Lifelong learning can enhance our understanding of the world, enabling more expansive opportunities and improved quality of life. In light of recent external impacts, there are resulting concerns for employers, including how they can stay competitive in the changing marketplace and attract and retain staff to meet the associated requirements. At the same time, there are also concerns for workers, including obtaining a job in a competitive employment landscape, remaining relevant, and retaining their job in light of the threats associated with globalization and automation. Therefore, if the societal attitude shifts to adopt lifelong learning successfully, it can significantly alleviate legitimate concerns for both businesses and individuals.

Lifelong Learning through the Eyes of the Employer

Because there are continuous updates to skills and knowledge and the rate of technological development is advancing rapidly, employers recognize that quality learning and development programs throughout their organizations are essential if they are going to keep the pace (Richardson & Richardson, 2017). While many workers will be taking it upon themselves to self-direct much of their ongoing development, there is a pressing need for employers to provide opportunities to develop their talent from within.

Static information is no longer relevant, and skills that were learned or knowledge obtained years ago have every chance of having been updated or even made obsolete. Therefore, it is unrealistic to expect that when an employee joins a company that the skills and knowledge they bring with them at that point in time will suffice throughout all their future years with the firm. Instead, employers can develop their workforce continuously through formal and informal learning to improve performance and expand growth opportunities.

Many workers are now looking for employers of choice who offer robust training programs and opportunities for development. Moreover, employees who realize their company is investing in their progress have been reported to be more likely to invest their own efforts back into the company in return.

Lifelong Learning through the Eyes of the Worker

The term worker is used here (and throughout many parts of the book) instead of employee, as this refers to all people who are in the workforce and not just those who are contractually attached to a single employer.

Because information, skills, and technologies are evolving at an increasingly rapid pace, most of these qualities may have a limited shelf life (Redmond & Macfadyen, 2020). In this era, skills must be maintained as a matter of necessity, and while workplaces can enable ongoing development, much of this learning also needs to be self-directed. Workers who remain relevant in today's workforce keep abreast of changes and seize opportunities to update their skills as an essential part of ongoing personal and professional development. Learning 'how to learn' is a skill that might take priority for many individuals as it enables workers to understand and put into practice the most effective methods for them to progress (Beaulieu et al., 2020).

Expanding one's outlook and education not only allows them to remain relevant in the workplace, but it can also enable internal, personal growth and often improved contribution to society (Eschenbacher & Fleming, 2020). Workers who regularly add education and skills to their resume stand out in a competitive employment landscape, and this can be as simple as utilizing readily available tools such as LinkedIn Learning's educational platform. LinkedIn Learning offers online courses which, once completed and assessed, can be added to the learner's public LinkedIn profile in the form of a verified badge (LinkedIn Learning, 2018; Moen, 2020).

Most importantly, however, lifelong learning can help to reduce the threat of job losses which is a reasonable concern for many as we move into a future that is enabled by automation. While advances in technology are in many ways responsible for these potential losses, they can also provide solutions for people to counteract and prevent such risks to their livelihoods.

Conclusion

All companies operating in today's fast-paced environment must accept changing customer expectations, technological trends, and increasingly flexible workforces and build accommodating learning structures to support them. To achieve balance and growth in an environment of continuous change, quality learning should be included at the core of all business strategies.

Lifelong learning is a strategic imperative in this volatile, complex, and ambiguous world. The ability to learn new skills and innovate during times of change is becoming more critical, and those who work within a culture of learning are more likely to adapt as their organizations pivot where necessary.

In light of such substantial impacts to work and learning, which are possibly more significant than ever before, it becomes critical that every person, team, leader, and workplace puts ongoing learning at the forefront of development.

Critical Thinking Questions

1   Digital technologies have revolutionized how we work. Why should technology-enhanced learning support this in the workplace?
2   In what ways has the COVID-19 pandemic impacted online workplace learning, and how will this effect online learning in the future?
3   If robotics and automation pose a threat to many current occupations, how can this be offset through lifelong learning?
4   Does globalization enable improved employment outcomes across the globe, or is it driving a further gap in equality?
5   Other than technology, globalization, the COVID-19 pandemic, the gig economy, and robotics, what external impacts are altering the way we need to learn?

References

Arnold, M. (2020). Book review: a very short, fairly interesting and reasonable cheap book about globalization. *Management Learning, 2002*, 1-4. DOI:10.1177/1350507620967636

Barbara, B., Brancatelli, R., Chumney, W., Dendinger, L., Nantz, B., Poepsel, M., & Shapiro, D. (2018). *Robotics, artificial intelligence, and the workplace of the future*. BC Campus Open Publishing. Retrieved from https://opentextbc.ca/businessethicsopenstax/chapter/robotics-artificial-intelligence-and-the-workplace-of-the-future/

Beaulieu, S., Frati, L., Miconi, T., Lehman, J., Stanley, K. O., Clune, J., & Cheney, N. (2020). Learning to continually learn. *arXiv preprint arXiv:2002.09571*.

Bennett, E. E., & McWhorter, R. R. (2021). Virtual HRD's role in crisis and the post covid-19 professional lifeworld: Accelerating skills for digital transformation. *Advances in Developing Human Resources, 23*(1), 5–25. DOI:10.1177/1523422320973288

Casper, W. J., & Buffardi, L. C. (2004). Work-life benefits and job pursuit intentions: The role of anticipated organizational support. *Journal of Vocational Behavior, 65*(3), 391-410. DOI:10.1016/j.jvb.2003.09.003

Dilmaghani, M. (2020). There is a time and a place for work: Comparative evaluation of flexible work arrangements in Canada. *International Journal of Manpower, 42*(1), 167–192. DOI:10.1108/IJM-12-2019-0555

Donorfio, L., & Chapman, B. (2020). Using technology to connect the generations and understand lifelong learning. *Innovation in Aging, 4*(Suppl 1), 554. DOI:10.1093/geroni/igaa057.1816

Eschenbacher, S., & Fleming, T. (2020). Transformative dimensions of lifelong learning: Mezirow, Rorty and COVID-19. *International Review of Education: Journal of Lifelong Learning, 66*(5–6), 657–672. DOI:10.1007/s11159-020-09859-6

European Commission (EC). (2001). *Making a European area of lifelong learning a reality*. Retrieved from https://epale.ec.europa.eu/en/resource-centre/content/making-european-area-lifelong-learning-reality-communication-commission-com

Grossman, R. (2015). *How to create a learning culture*. The Society for Human Resource Management. Retrieved from https://www.shrm.org/hr-today/news/hr-magazine/Pages/0515-learning-culture.aspx

Harari, Y. (2019). *21 lessons for the 21st Century*. London: Random House.

Joy, S., & Kolb, D. A. (2009). Are there cultural differences in learning style?. *International Journal of Intercultural Relations, 33*(1), 69–85. DOI:10.1016/j.ijintrel.2008.11.002

Kelly, K. (2017). *The inevitable – understanding the 12 technological forces that will shape our future*. New York: Penguin Group.

LinkedIn Learning (2018). 2018 workplace learning report: The rise and responsibility of talent development in training systems and tools in the new labor market. Retrieved from https://learning.linkedin.com

London, M. (Ed.). (2011). *The Oxford handbook of lifelong learning*. London: Oxford University Press.

McKinsey and Company. (2020). *The State of AI in 2020*. Retrieved from https://www.mckinsey.com/business-functions/mckinsey-analytics/our-insights/global-survey-the-state-of-ai-in-2020

Merriam-Webster Dictionary. (2021). Globalization. *Merriam-webster.com dictionary*. Retrieved from https://www.merriam-webster.com/dictionary/globalization

Moen, M. H. (2020). Media smart libraries: Digital badges for professional learning. In M. H. Moen & Buchanan, S. A. (Eds.), *Leading professional development: Growing librarians for the digital age* (pp. 29–38). California: ABC-CLIO, Inc.

Nath, D., Sridhar, V., Adya, M., & Malik, A. (2010). *Project quality of offshore virtual teams engaged in software requirements analysis: An exploratory comparative study*. IGI Global.

Nguyen, J. (2020). *A human's guide to the future*. Pan McMillan: Australia.

Oxford Online Dictionary (2021). Gig economy. *Oxford Learners' Dictionary*. www.oxfordlearnersdictionaries.com/definition/english/gig-economy

Ramalingam, S., & Mahalingam, A. (2011). Enabling conditions for the emergence and effective performance of technical and cultural boundary spanners in global virtual teams. *Engineering Project Organization Journal, 1*(2), 121–141. DOI:10.1080/21573727.2011.572964

Redmond, W. D., & Macfadyen, L. P. (2020). A framework to leverage and mature learning ecosystems. *International Journal of Emerging Technologies in Learning, 15*(5), 75–99. DOI:10.3991/ijet.v15i05.11898

Rensink, I. (2016). *Cultural differences in work-related learning: A cross-cultural comparison of self-directedness and (in) formal learning activities* [master's thesis, University of Twente]. University of Twente Student Theses. Retrieved from https://essay.utwente.nl/70879/

Richardson, T. M., & Richardson, E. (2017). Aligning people and purpose. In *The Toyota engagement equation: How to understand and implement continuous improvement thinking in any organization* (1st ed.). New York: McGraw-Hill Education.

Shivakumar, S. K. (2020). Digital workplace case study. In *Build a next-generation digital workplace* (pp. 173–198). New York: Apress.

Short, H., & Greener, S. (2014). TEL in the workplace. *British Journal of Educational Technology, 45*(6), 983–989. DOI:10.1111/bjet.12213

Stephany, F., Dunn, M., Sawyer, S., & Lehdonvirta, V. (2020). Distancing bonus or downscaling loss? The changing livelihood of us online workers in times of COVID-19. *Tijdschrift voor economische en sociale geografie, 11*(3), 561–573. DOI:10.1111/tesg.12455

Totterdill, P. (2013, December 5). *Workplace innovation: the fifth element [Video] YouTube*. Retrieved from https://www.youtube.com/watch?v=hutLABOniCc

Vallas, S., & Schor, J. B. (2020). What do platforms do? Understanding the gig economy. *Annual Review of Sociology, 46*, 273–294. DOI:10.1146/annurev-soc-121919-054857

Chapter 2

Learning and Development: Evolution and Impacts

Learning and development (L&D) in the workplace is a rapidly maturing function that has evolved from somewhat of a compliance and accreditation operation to one that actively and purposefully drives continuous improvement across an organization. Modern L&D teams lead strategic projects that reach far beyond traditional onboarding and occupational safety programs.

Following the COVID-19 pandemic, workforces may remain at least partially remote, meaning that L&D professionals will be dealing with a new set of challenges, particularly regarding ensuring workers have equitable access to online and blended learning opportunities. Maintaining connected, digitally literate teams has become a training priority, not to mention the revised focus on communication protocols, cybersecurity, mental well-being, and the new COVID-19 safe work practices. It's time for L&D professionals to take a leading role in establishing these sustainable programs while at the same time ensuring the continuous growth, development, and improvement of talent throughout the organization.

This chapter examines some of the significant events that have impacted the role of L&D over recent times. These include organizational transformations, the improved technology landscape, the

DOI: 10.1201/9781003149132-3

technology-enabled integration of work and training, the alterations to instructional design, the culture shift to continuous learning, and engagement in the workplace.

Note – for the purpose of clarity throughout this chapter, the term learning and development (L&D) will refer to all learning functions and operations within a workplace. The titles Learning and Development Specialist and Learning and Development Professional are used interchangeably. These act as umbrella descriptions to include all roles related to learning within an organization. These include, but are not limited to, Chief Learning Officer, Learning and Development Manager, Instructional Designer, Learning Designer, Learning Analyst, Learning Management System Administrator, Learning Advisor, Education Specialist, Talent Developer, and Learning Partner.

Organizational Transformation

As discussed in Chapter 1, organizations are undergoing some of the most significant transformations in history. These transformations are occurring, willingly or not, due to technology, globalization, the COVID-19 pandemic, the gig economy, and the rise of robotics. Because of such impacts, an increasing number of L&D professionals are taking a seat at the table of strategic planning meetings to ensure the required knowledge and skills are identified and aligned with company goals.

As workers are at the heart of organizational transformations, upskilling and supporting them during these unpredictable times is vital. Sophisticated change management and well-planned training programs ensure the required knowledge and skills are in place as changes unfold. However, in many instances, organizational transformations will regrettably fail because the workforce is not fully informed on the changes or how to alter their knowledge and skill-sets accordingly.

It is crucial not only for the company to value learning as an ongoing process (Daneshgari & Moore, 2016) but also for the individual. Modgil (2020) claims that we can expect a steady decline in permanent jobs as the gig economy modifies the future of work. Working in the gig economy requires adaptability and innovation and certainly requires continuous training to keep skills current and relevant. Training can no longer be considered one-and-done, as technological advancements are ongoing, and L&D professionals are tasked with ensuring the entire workforce is developed, not just the permanent employees. This may be alarming considering a survey conducted by Price, Waterhouse Coopers that revealed widespread CEO concern of their organization's ability to improve and innovate. They claim this is because they are hindered by a lack of critical skills among their workers (and this was only taking into account the permanent employees). In addition to this, McDonough (2017) claims that American employers have long warned about the economic consequences of the current skills gap across the workforce and highlight the importance of developing new strategies to improve worker's fundamental skills. This suggests that in many ways, it is not just the organizations that are transforming; it is the entire workforce and the economy as well.

Moreover, as the world becomes more connected and social environments change, the general nature of work and the modern workplace's skill requirements are also changing (Gerick, Eickelmann, & Bos, 2017). Therefore, the skills and knowledge taught in the workplace need to adapt accordingly. Business practices that may have worked in the past may no longer work in the post-pandemic, globalized future, and persisting with brute force will only exhaust workers and resources (Daneshgari & Moore, 2016). Instead, learning new ways and incorporating revised and innovative practices can allow organizations and their workers to adapt and thrive. When individuals can develop and embrace incremental change and continuous development, they can create an atmosphere that extends from the individual to the team, from the team to other teams, and eventually to the whole organization. When these transformational virtues can be led or 'rolled out' from the top, authenticity grows and develops within the workers.

Overall, the impact that organizational transformation is having on the future of L&D in the workplace is substantial. As processes and services change, along with the ways of working and operating, the learning curve for all individuals becomes significant and ongoing. By aligning the company's mission and vision to its workers' training goals (Figure 2.1), opportunities are presented to expand capabilities and invest in its sustainability and growth. These contribute to the worker's professional development, targeted training programs and career progression.

Figure 2.1   Improved outcomes facilitated by the alignment of goals.

The Improved Technology Landscape

The advancement of digital technologies in the workplace and beyond is nothing short of incredible. Employees are often enabled to work agilely, collaboratively, and securely using digital tools that continue to expand, offering more valuable and improved functionality.

> Many companies are aware that the pace and scale of technological advancement needs to be matched with the speed and scale of learning programs to keep up with innovation and continuous change (De Smet, Patchod, Relyea, & Sterndels, 2020). At the same time, these digital trends enable businesses to automate much of their lower-skilled work so that employees can focus on higher-level tasks. (Lopes, Scully-Russ, Zarestky, & Collins, 2020).

This advancing technological landscape impacts the role of L&D in two ways:

1. The use of workplace technology drives the education required. That is, the general use of technology across the workplace results in workers' continuous requirement to be trained. This includes all digital tools that update, evolve, and expand over time.
2. Technologies such as the core learning management system (LMS) enables education to be delivered. Workplace learning is enhanced by a variety of digital tools that are growing exponentially. The ability to leverage artificial intelligence, immersive technologies, and adaptive educational experiences, along with a multitude of content offerings, are made possible within advanced learning management systems.

The LMS hosts digital workplace training initiatives, working as a central point for learning technologies. From storing and delivering course materials to tracking, assessment, and communication, LMSs provide the foundations for many complex learning initiatives (Balogh & Turčáni, 2011), and in recent times these technologies have progressed dramatically (Figure 2.2).

The LMS has technically been in use for around 100 years, but it wasn't until the 1950s when it was actively used as a tool to learn asynchronously through the University of Houston that it started to take form. The university uploaded lesson content that was available to students in the evenings so they could attend work during the day and still be allowed to study (Athmika, 2020). This was a revolutionary idea at the time, but little further progress was made until 1983, when Project Athena was introduced. This was a networked computer system designed to serve the academic community's needs across the Massachusetts Institute of Technology campus (MIT,) and paved the way for the extensive use of the LMS.

However, the most explosive development was in the early 2000s, when Moodle and other popular LMS platforms were introduced, catapulting the LMS into the more flexible, user-friendly, and integrative applications we experience today. In addition to these new systems, the introduction of SCORM improved the experience by providing

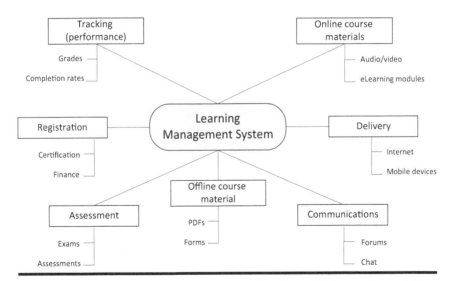

Figure 2.2   Learning management systems in the workplace. Adapted from Balogh and Turčáni (2011).

standards for developing content. SCORM's successor xAPI arrived on the scene in 2013 (Rouse, 2019), which further opened up the possibility to integrate several different systems to deliver and track more complex learning data. Overall, the LMS has dramatically evolved over the past decade from being a tool used to share course documents and upload assessment tasks, to a dynamic and robust environment that supports collaborative, flexible, and personalized learning (Mershad & Wakim, 2018). (Beyond this, we start to look at the more modern Learning Experience Platforms discussed further in Chapter 8).

With access to sophisticated learning management systems and their integrated tools, workplace education can be effectively managed, but the software on its own does not deliver the outcomes. The design of the content and development pathways within them lies with carefully skilled L&D specialists who can plan, design, execute, and evaluate effective ongoing training programs. What we access today is a vast choice of instructional mediums that can deliver, assess, and track education that occurs in various contexts. This expanding field brings more and more offers to the market every year that can be included in comprehensive learning programs. Much of the previous work involved in creating content from scratch has been eliminated with the ability to explore and curate content from a wide variety of sources.

The improved technology landscape, and more specifically, the enhanced LMS and accompanying digital tools, have brought about an advancement of online learning that is interactive, motivating, targeted, and often self-directed. With the ability to analyze data to track, manage, and predict outcomes, we now have the opportunity to define ambitious goals and source the experiences that enable them.

The Technology-Enabled Integration of Work and Learning

Traditionally, workplace learning took on a linear approach and was either (1) accomplished before starting work at the organization, for example, obtaining a university degree, or (2) carried out offsite, requiring a worker to 'down tools' for a day or two and attend an instructor lead training course. Times have changed, and now L&D professionals are increasingly able to facilitate opportunities while on the job or in the workplace. Technology-enhanced integration of work and learning refers to the ways in which technology can be used as a tool to enable education in or alongside daily working activities.

Throughout the COVID-19 pandemic, most of the workforce, including the most accomplished leaders, had to undergo a steep learning curve as they adjusted to their new ways of working. They needed to learn how to deal with crises, make decisions at a faster pace, learn new systems, and develop new skills. There was reduced time for formal instruction, and opportunities needed to be embedded quickly into daily work routines. Learning on the job unfolded as a matter of necessity, and those who were able to learn rapidly and effectively were fortunate enough to have a competitive edge. As a result, companies began to develop metacognitive, digital literacy, and critical thinking skills at many levels within their organization. This accelerates their employees' capacity to learn new things, engage effectively with technology and develop relevant skills for the future (De Smet et al., 2020).

It may be some time before we can effectively evaluate the L&D that has taken place during the pandemic. Still, it would be reasonably safe to assume that as we were collectively pushed to learn on the job, it became evident that this approach can be successful with the proper uptake of technology and online learning. It has, however, brought to light the relatively sparse body of historical research on the technology-enhanced integration of work and learning. Ley (2020) carried out studies on the content published within the British Journal of Educational Technology and noted that despite the journal recognizing the importance of technology-enhanced learning within the workplace, the journal's research focuses primarily on formal education settings. A similar, earlier evaluation on journal editions between 2000 and 2005 also revealed that only 3% of publications featured research conducted in the workplace (Latchem, 2006).

More recently, due to the COVID-19 pandemic and subsequent lockdowns, the focus has quickly shifted into this area. Vargo, Zhu, Benwell, and Yan (2021) note that they reviewed 260 articles examining the varieties of digital technologies used during the pandemic (many of them used for learning and instruction). While the main focus of the article was on healthcare, school-based education, and the general use of technology in the workplace, it highlights the enormous new interest in the space. It will potentially lead to expansive studies specifically focused on digitally supported training in the workplace.

Ley (2020) depicts his views on the integration of work and learning by identifying what he describes as 'knowledge structures.' These structures represent how workplace concepts such as business process descriptions, domain vocabularies, and competency descriptions are interrelated, embedded in social networks and similar formalizations (Figure 2.3).

These knowledge structures can be created through discussion, modeling, and validation among stakeholders who are experts with the content and represent a snapshot of how the organizational community understands their domain and the skills required to perform their roles (Ley, 2020). The contextual nature of such structures depends on where it takes place. For example, in highly socialized domains, such as within the construction or healthcare industries, the workplace addresses things differently to those in more autonomous professions (Ley, 2020). Therefore, significant time needs to be spent understanding how the domain operates, which digital technologies are in use, and the constraints and opportunities that exist before determining learning interventions (Ley et al., 2014).

Regardless of the skills and knowledge to be acquired, L&D specialists have far more reach than they previously did when it comes to integrating training into the workplace. As the global pandemic taught us, learning often needs to be undertaken at a rapid pace, and with access to digital technologies, we can deliver such experiences as required. However, whatever learning is happening in the

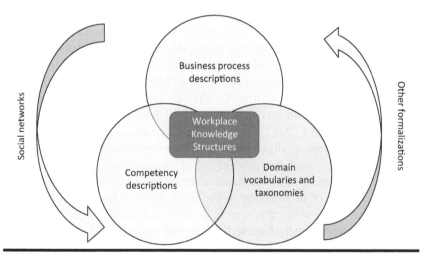

Figure 2.3   Workplace knowledge structures. Adapted from Ley (2020).

workplace, it doesn't occur in a silo. It is essential to consider environmental factors such as management support, reliable access to technology, workload and priorities, peer support, and the opportunity to incorporate new skills into practice.

The Alterations to Instructional Design

Instructional design is the practice of systematically designing, developing, and delivering educational experiences. These experiences are usually blended between physical and digital mediums and are delivered in a variety of ways. Traditionally, instructional designers (which in the workplace can often be a role taken on by a number of different L&D practitioners) were responsible for the end-to-end design of a learning program, including analysis, design, development, implementation, and evaluation.

However, instructional design is becoming much more complex and comprehensive. When the COVID-19 pandemic pushed the closure of businesses across the globe, it forced workers to (1) learn new ways of working and (2) learn online through digital mediums. From the instructional designer's perspective, this altered the precision and speed of analysis, design, development, and implementation, often leading to short-cuts and add-ons that don't fit the organization's needs. In addition to this, many businesses don't have dedicated Instructional Designers who can successfully carry out these functions and have either outsourced the design of their learning programs or muddled through as best they could.

Currently, the sheer depth and breadth of learning experiences required and the need for them to be delivered online means that traditional frameworks for instructional design may need to be reconsidered. Firstly, there is the mess that needs to be cleaned up, which was the sudden ad hoc learning solutions that were implemented when the pandemic struck. Secondly, the knowledge and skills that need to be impressed could be very different from what they were before, meaning that many off-the-shelf learning solutions need to be revised, and the sequencing and focus of content should also be evaluated. Thirdly, decision-makers need to become aware of the importance of effective learning design and the investment required in the digital technology that enables it. At present, we have inconsistent band-aid solutions strewn across industries, and these need to be brought together to define new concepts and new frameworks specific to the workplace. Hopefully, this will bring successful and mature instructional design to the next level.

The Culture of Continuous Learning

"Continuous learning is the process of learning new skills and knowledge on an ongoing basis. This can come in many forms, from formal course taking to informal social learning. It involves self-initiative and taking on challenges" (Valamis, n.d). It encompasses a mindset that accepts new ideas, faces challenges, and actively solves problems.

It has long been recognized that education shouldn't be restricted to formal, uniform processes that stop after graduating with a degree or completing an apprenticeship. It would be reasonable to assume that most education occurs after this point. As a result, if an organization isn't continuously exposing its workers to learning experiences, they risk falling behind those who keep the pace.

Complacency, which is in contrast to continuous L&D (Wood & Lynch Jr., 2002), can drag companies and their employees down, wasting resources and innovation and yielding poor results from both an individual perspective and that of the broader team. Ideally, continuous learning cultures have vibrant and energized teams who support each other in their ongoing learning journeys, leading to feelings of accomplishment, ownership of outcomes, and looking for new ways to improve and share knowledge with peers (Figure 2.4).

L&D specialists and other leaders within the company can encourage a culture of continuous learning by fostering the following practices as outlined by Norman (2018).

1. Assess the current strengths and weaknesses of employees across the company.
2. Allocate mentors to mentees and other collaborative groups.
3. Utilize the organization's learning materials and tools and source quality external resources to fill any gaps.
4. Encourage the workforce to take their learning further by allocating time and funds to ongoing training opportunities.
5. Lead by example, demonstrating behaviors and beliefs that align with a culture of ongoing learning. This is particularly useful when senior managers and leaders across the organization demonstrate a similar commitment.

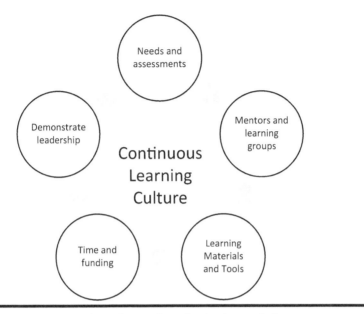

Figure 2.4   The culture of continuous learning in the workplace.

In addition to this, the key to building this type of culture is to provide the educational experiences that workers require. Because today's jobs are usually more demanding, time-poor, and more potential knowledge could be incorporated, training needs to be targeted to fit in when time is available. When learning experiences are rich, concise, and engaging, individuals are more likely to invest their time into activities that will yield positive outcomes for their professional performance.

While it is a positive sign that many workers are undertaking their own educational initiatives, L&D professionals are usually better equipped to determine which experiences will provide the best outcomes. They can identify opportunities that are credible, trustworthy, current, relevant, and high quality. However, rather than discouraging individuals from seeking out their own opportunities, L&D practitioners can coach them on how to best source and evaluate their options (Fenwick, 2008).

Collaboration is also encouraged within a culture of continuous learning as this will assist in transferring employee knowledge and capabilities in an informal context. Knowledge and information are shared during the act of collaboration, which can positively impact the individuals and the company. However, there are two things to consider when it comes to collaboration activities (including mentoring) that support workplace learning. The first is workplace diversity, and the second is the controversial but unavoidable topic of ego.

According to Zajac (2017), despite many organizations' best efforts to create inclusive environments that support diversity in the workplace, they often struggle to achieve this. She states that employees from all ethnicities, races, genders, political views, religions, and sexual orientations should feel comfortable, respected, and like they can contribute. This is particularly relevant when collaborating and transferring knowledge. Lopes et al. (2020) explain that there is an increased need for improved soft skills in the workplace because of the increase in diversity. Soft skill training is gaining traction and is an essential part of comprehensive training. However, Yadzinski and Nakatsu (2020) suggest that the term soft skills may infer something lesser than hard skills because of the word 'soft.' Hard skills are perceived as more technical and tangible, leading to the belief that they may be more valuable. This suggests there is work to be done in this area if we are to truly foster cultures of collaboration and continuous learning.

The other thing to take into account is ego. Griffin and Burns (2018) explain in their book *The Learning Imperative: Raising Performance in Organisations by Improving Learning* that successful learners need to balance their own egotistical needs with the drive for collective growth. They claim to have seen, time and again, that team learning grinds to a halt because of the impact of unhealthy egos, which can undermine relationships, trust, and collaboration. Moreover, it is interesting to note that Yang and Maxwell (2011) claim there are some instances where employees do not want to contribute information as they see that knowledge as something they've earned and is valuable to their role in the company. These individuals often prioritize their desire to outdo others and place it above the group's collective needs (Griffin & Burns, 2018). Therefore, when designing learning opportunities that involve collaboration and teamwork, it is vital to consider the impacts of diversity and ego. While they receive relatively little attention, neither should be taken lightly.

The internal learning culture in the workplace is structured by the overall attitude toward learning and technology. According to Abdullah, Ziden, Aman, and Mustafa (2015), learning outcomes largely depend on the learner's mindset. Two aspects may drive these attitudes, which are: (1) The learner's affective thinking. This relates to the individual's comfort level using technology, leading to potential

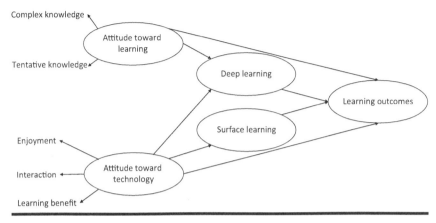

Figure 2.5 Learning outcomes influenced by learner attitudes. Adapted from Lee and Choi (2017).

feelings of anxiety or enjoyment. (2) The learner's cognitive thinking. This relates to the degree that the individual believes the technology enhances their learning experience (Agyei & Voogt, 2011). As a result, the learner's attitude, whether driven by affective or cognitive thinking, effects their experience with learning technologies, and ultimately their learning outcomes (Gregory & Lodge, 2015). Therefore, technology-enhanced learning programs benefit by addressing these issues and embedding them as part of the program (Figure 2.5).

Employee Engagement

Employee engagement is indicative of an individual's commitment to their organization and the enthusiasm and genuine effort they put into their job. High levels of engagement can be attributed to many factors ranging from the company culture to an individual's character, personal values, and aspirations. Engaged workers are usually of higher value to their company, and they also experience more job satisfaction (Khan, Md. Yusoff, Hussain, & Ismail, 2019) and quality of life while at work. At an organizational level, engagement is essential so that employees enthusiastically contribute to outcomes, promote company values, and support those around them.

It has been noted that the companies that have substantial levels of employee engagement understand that investment in training and development contributes to this. When employees participate in ongoing training programs, mainly when they are involved in designing their learning plans, the results are higher productivity, more innovation, and improved company culture. When employees note that their employer cares about their development, it is likely to build respect, motivation, and loyalty.

Measuring employee engagement can show what things are working and where improvements can be made. Metrics such as turnover rates, absenteeism, net promoter scores, and employee engagement surveys can provide high-level data, but within individual teams, their managers should be monitoring results, key performance indicators, participation, and communication (Hossen, Chan, & Hasan, 2020). We are likely to see a sharp rise in the adoption of technologies that map employee engagement, progress, and emotional connection to a company. These technologies range from human resource management software to social media engagement.

Employees who feel their company has invested in their development feel valued and empowered, and this shouldn't be restricted to potential leaders. Workers who can see results from their training will be engaged. This includes recognition, application, and self-realization of the benefits occurring from utilizing their new skills. The opportunity to share knowledge also reinforces what has been learned and the opportunities for further development. It's time to question past practices and implement new designs. This may take a lot of education for all levels of the organization, but it leads to genuine ownership and engagement that drives strong businesses into the future.

It is increasingly recognized that training in the workplace is a continuous practice that involves ongoing and engaging educational opportunities. As a result, the L&D function is expanding to provide far greater exposure and more thoughtfully designed programs than in times gone past.

Conclusion

In conclusion, L&D in the workplace has significantly progressed in recent decades and continues to rapidly evolve. External impacts such as globalization, the gig economy, and technological advancements have affected how people work and have also raised individuals' expectations to learn continuously throughout their lives. It is no longer acceptable for L&D teams to be merely responsible for only onboarding and annual compliance training. Instead, the L&D function needs to lead from the middle, aligning robust training programs with company goals and strategies. Organizations should be developing learning visions that are communicated clearly to all levels of the company.

L&D teams are also growing and expanding from performing the roles of trainers and instructional designers to creating new roles that have strong skills in change management, learning analytics, and program development. These teams work closely with a range of other departments, including ICT, HR, and external providers, to ensure the best outcomes for the business and its workforce. At present, it is common for L&D teams to sit within the human resource department, and this too may evolve as its future potential is realized. In the same way that ICT was originally commonly placed as a subdepartment of finance (for reasons one can only assume were that they had nowhere else to sit), they have now grown and formed large departments in their own right. The same may transpire for the future of L&D, as teams expand to include multiple roles such as program managers, project managers, instructional designers, learning analysts, learning applications specialists, LMS administrators, and so on.

Aligning with this changing workplace, the L&D professional's role is also expanding as they reshape the capabilities of the organization. Organizations that prioritize L&D as a critical function see improvements in the caliber of employees they attract and also increase retention rates, employee engagement, and their reputation as an employer of choice.

As we emerge from the COVID-19 pandemic, many businesses are forever altered, resulting in a dire need to reskill, upskill, and revaluate practices. Consequently, L&D professionals are now dealing with a new set of challenges that are more expansive than ever before. Throughout this chapter, we examined some of the significant events that have impacted the role of L&D over recent times, noting that organizational transformations are occurring due to several factors. This transformation results in a steep learning curve for almost all of the workforce as they regroup and refocus on new ways of working.

The improved technology landscape has resulted in superior business and educational tools, including more sophisticated learning management systems. With the ability to integrate data and offer a wide variety of materials and pathways, L&D managers have an exciting but very large task ahead of them. In addition to this, the culture shift to continuous development is increasingly accepted and encouraged within the workplace, meaning there is far greater exposure to educational opportunities in daily life.

Finally, the individual ownership of learning outcomes has impacted L&D operations in how ongoing training has become not only accepted but expected, resulting in significant avenues for professional development and overall company growth. A clear shift is occurring, resulting in the collective realization of the importance that learning holds. Hopefully, moving into the future, more organizations elevate L&D and invest in robust and ongoing training programs that will propel them into the future.

Critical Thinking Questions

1   Learning management systems are the most common platforms used to deliver and monitor online learning. How can these technologies be further enhanced to support workplace development?
2   The development of metacognitive skills, digital literacy, and critical thinking enables individuals to learn more quickly. How can these skills be incorporated into ongoing learning opportunities in the workplace?
3   How can knowledge structures within an organization be effectively documented, shared, and updated using digital technology?
4   Where should learning and development teams sit within an organizational structure, and why?
5   What are the comparisons between learning and development in the 2000s to the 2020s? How might this change further in the coming decade?

References

Abdullah, Z. D., Ziden, A. B. A., Aman, R. B. C., & Mustafa, K. I. (2015). Students' attitudes towards information technology and the relationship with their academic achievement. *Contemporary Education Technology*, 6(4), 338e354.

Agyei, D. D., & Voogt, J. M. (2011). Exploring the potential of the will, skill, tool model in Ghana: Predicting prospective and practicing teachers' use of technology. *Computers & Education*, 56(1), 91e100. DOI:10.1016/j.compedu.2010.08.017

Athmika, T. (2020). *A brief history of the learning management system (LMS)*. Commlab India. Retrieved from https://blog.commlabindia.com/elearning-design/learning-management-system-evolution

Balogh, Z., & Turčáni, M. (2011). Possibilities of modelling web-based education using IF-THEN rules and fuzzy petri nets in LMS. In *International conference on informatics engineering and information science* (pp. 93–106). Springer, Berlin, Heidelberg. Retrieved from https://link. springer.com/chapter/10.1007/978-3-642-25327-0_9

Daneshgari, P., & Moore, H. (2016). Organizational transformation through improved employee engagement– "How to use effective methodologies to improve business productivity and expand market share." *Strategic HR Review, 15*(2), 57–64. DOI:10.1108/HR-02-2016-0007

De Smet, A., Patchod, D., Relyea, C., & Sterndels, B. (2020). Ready, set, go: Reinventing the organization for speed in the post-COVID-19 era. *McKinsey Quarterly Magazine [Internet].* Retrieved July 20, 2020, from https://www.mckinsey.com/business-functions/organization/our-insights/ready-set-go-reinventing-the-organization-for-speed-in-the-post-covid-19-era

Fenwick, T. (2008). Workplace learning: Emerging trends and new perspectives. *New Directions for Adult and Continuing Education, 2008*, 17–26. DOI:10.1002/ace.302

Gerick, J., Eickelmann, B., & Bos, W. (2017). School-level predictors for the use of ICT in schools and students' CIL in international comparison. *Large-scale Assessments in Education, 5*(1), 1–13. DOI:10.1186/s40536-017-0037-7

Gregory, M., & Lodge, J. (2015). Academic workload: The silent barrier to the implementation of technology-enhanced learning strategies in higher education. *Distance Education, 36*(2), 201e230.

Griffin, M., & Burns, A. (2018). *The learning imperative: raising performance in organizations by improving learning.* Wales, UK: Crown House Publishing.

Hossen, M. M., Tak-Jie Chan, & Hasan, N. A. M. (2020). Mediating role of job satisfaction on internal corporate social responsibility practices and employee engagement in higher education sector. *Contemporary Management Research, 16*(3), 207–227. DOI:10.7903/cmr.20334

Khan, M. A., Md. Yusoff, R., Hussain, A., & Ismail, F. (2019). The mediating effect of job satisfaction on the relationship of HR practices and employee job performance: Empirical evidence from higher education sector. *International Journal of Organizational Leadership, 8*, 78–94. DOI:10.33844/ijol.2019.60392

Latchem, C. (2006). Editorial: A content analysis of the British Journal of Educational Technology. *British Journal of Educational Technology, 37*(4), 503–511. DOI:10.1111/j.1467-8535.2006.00635.x

Lee, J., & Choi, H. (2017). What affects learner's higher-order thinking in technology-enhanced learning environments? The effects of learner factors. *Computers & Education, 115*(1) 143–152. i). Contents lists available at ScienceDirect Computers & Education journal homepage: www.elsevier.com/locate/compedu doi:10.1016/j.compedu.2017.06.015

Ley, T. (2020). Knowledge structures for integrating working and learning: A reflection on a decade of learning technology research for workplace learning. *British Journal of Educational Technology, 51*(2), 331–346. DOI:10.1111/bjet.12835

Ley, T., Cook, J., Dennerlein, S., Kravcik, M., Kunzmann, C., Pata, K., & Trattner, C. (2014). Scaling informal learning at the workplace: A model and four designs from a large-scale design-based research effort. *British Journal of Educational Technology, 45*(6), 1036–1048. DOI:10.1111/bjet.12197

Lopes, T., Scully-Russ, E., Zarestky, J., & Collins, J. C. (2020). The effects of social characteristics of jobs on adults' cognitive skills in the United States: A PIAAC analysis. *Adult Education Quarterly, 70*(2), 140–174. DOI:10.1177/0741713619884567

McDonough, T. (2017). Closing the skills gap: Key learnings for employers and job seekers. *Employment Relations Today, 43*(4), 49–54. DOI:10.1002/ert.21602

Mershad, K., & Wakim, P. (2018). A learning management system enhanced with the internet of things applications. *Journal of Education and Learning, 7*(3), 23–40. DOI:10.5539/jel.v7n3p23

MIT (n.d.). *Athena history (1983 – present) from A to Z*. Massachusetts Institute of Technology. Retrieved from http://web.mit.edu/acs/athena.html

Modgil, S. (2020). *Imagining the new normal: The great organizational overhaul*. People Matters Global. Retrieved from https://www.peoplemattersglobal.com/article/strategic-hr/imagining-the-new-normal-the-great-organizational-overhaul-26109

Norman, J. (2018). How leaders build a culture of continuous learning in the workplace. *Assessments 24×7*. Retrieved from https://www.assessments24x7.com/blog/culture-of-continuous-learning

Price Waterhouse Coopers. (2019). *22nd annual global CEO survey*. Price Waterhouse Coopers. Retrieved from https://www.pwc.com/gx/en/ceo-survey/2019/report/pwc-22nd-annual-global-ceo-survey.pdf

Rouse, A. (2019). *The decline and fall of SCORM and why you should care*. LinkedIn. Retrieved from https://www.linkedin.com/pulse/decline-fall-scorm-why-you-should-care-amy-rouse

Wasson, B., & Kirschner, P. A. (2020). Learning design: European approaches. *TechTrends, 64*(6), 815–827. DOI:10.1007/s11528-020-00498-0

Valamis. (n.d.). *Continuous learning*. Valamis. Retrieved from https://www.valamis.com/hub/continuous-learning

Van Merriënboer, J., & Kirschner, P. (2018). *Ten steps to complex learning* (3rd ed.). New York: Taylor & Francis.

Vargo, D., Zhu, L., Benwell, B., & Yan, Z. (2021). Digital technology use during COVID-19 pandemic: A rapid review. *Human Behavior and Emerging Technologies, 3*(1), 13–24. DOI:10.1002/hbe2.242

Wood, S. L., & Lynch Jr., J. G. (2002). Prior knowledge and complacency in new product learning. *Journal of Consumer Research*, *29*(3), 416–426. DOI:10.2139/ssrn.339383

Yadzinski, S., & Nakatsu, T. (2020). How immersive learning technology is transforming workforce training and driving social impact. *Jobs 4 the Future*. Retrieved from https://jobs4thefuture.medium.com/how-immersive-learning-technology-is-transforming-workforce-training-and-driving-social-impact-9060ada6182b

Yang, T. M., & Maxwell, T. A. (2011). Information-sharing in public organizations: A litera- ture review of interpersonal, intra-organizational and inter-organizational success factors. *Government Information Quarterly*, *28*, 164–175.

Zajac, L. (2017). The necessary evolution of diversity & inclusion: The three "Rs" (recognition, relationships and respect for all) critical to building a truly inclusive workplace. *International In-House Counsel Journal*, *11*(45), 1–8.

Chapter 3

Eight Learning Imperatives

In recent times, workplace learning opportunities have made rapid advancements that have been driven by several forces. The two most significant of these are the development and scope of digital technologies and the impact of the COVID-19 pandemic on the global workforce. Since the onset of the pandemic, organizations have been forced to make major changes, often requiring employees to work remotely, utilizing digital collaboration platforms and other online tools. As a result, companies and individuals alike have undergone steep learning curves. This chapter defines eight learning imperatives that have come into focus and may assist in facilitating online learning. These learning imperatives are adaptability, engagement, flexibility, personalization, accessibility, social learning, meaningful assessment, and relevance. Each of these learning imperatives is explored through the lens of technological advancement and the future of workplace learning.

Adaptability

Merriam-Webster (2020) defines adaptability as the ability *"to change or be changed to fit or work better in some situation or for some purpose,"* which couldn't be more relevant than in the post-pandemic

DOI: 10.1201/9781003149132-4   **47**

workplace. Adaptability is required as organizations experience rapid change and workplaces continue to adjust to their heavily impacted and volatile environments. Individuals and organizations that foster adaptable practices can respond more effectively to the changing conditions around them (Calarco & Gurvis, 2006). When discussing adaptability in the context of an imperative for online learning, there are three aspects to consider:

1. Adaptable skills

Adaptable skills can be described as flexible skillsets that can be adapted across various settings (i.e., technology, communication, and problem-solving skills).

2. Adaptable mindsets

Adaptable mindsets feature positive outlooks and attitudes toward changing and reskilling where necessary (i.e., being open to new ideas and ways of working).

3. Adaptable learning resources

Adaptable learning resources include the design of learning programs and resources that can be adjusted to meet the needs of various learning mediums. (i.e., providing content available in a variety of formats such as written text, audio, and video).

Adaptable Skills

Implementing skills that can be adapted across various settings usually focuses on soft skills or technology skills that can be used in multiple roles and situations. Soft skills help people work together, think creatively, and see things through a critical lens (Calarco & Gurvis, 2006), while technology skills assist with communication, presentation, and operational functions.

When employees learn the types of skills that can be adapted to most business situations, they are better equipped to fulfill their role and feel confident in doing so. People with robust, adaptable skillsets learn new concepts quicker, transfer skills and knowledge to different situations, and tend to think more critically. Adaptable skills are a requirement that is here to stay, and so long as we see the ever-changing nature of information and ICT innovations accelerating, there will be further need for adaptable skills among workers (MacGregor, 2005).

Adaptable Mindsets

By encouraging positive attitudes toward being adaptable, workers become more accepting of the workplace's ever-changing nature. Adaptable attitudes include the willingness to try new things, being curious, and experimental, and taking creative approaches toward solving problems. People with adaptable mindsets feel it's ok to make mistakes and build on their skills over time; they demonstrate resilience and are recognized as being more resourceful.

Positive attitudes toward being adaptable means that challenges and changes are embraced, and people remain relevant throughout their working lives. Adaptable leaders understand that change is constant. They keep teams and employees motivated and focused on what is coming next, never finding themselves stuck in old ways of doing things. They realize that there are many solutions to problems and innovative new ideas that can be found in many places. This is why continuous learning and development is key to business success and why ongoing learning programs also need to be adaptable to individual ways of learning and working.

According to Brown (2017), when individuals learn to adapt through personal experiences and their reflection on them, they can construct their own internal understanding of new practices. He outlines some activities to encourage this, such as peer support, weekly case reviews, and mentoring, which can all enhance an individual's attitude toward adaptability.

Adaptable Learning Resources

There are many studies to support the fact that learning is best supported through a variety of means. For example, Dual Coding Theory (Clark & Paivio, 1991) states information is processed in the brain through two independent channels, and for this reason, it is important to include multiple formats of data. The left hemisphere of the brain is more analytical and processes verbal information such as text and audio. Whereas the brain's right hemisphere is more creative and processes visual information such as videos, images, and charts. Therefore, providing instruction via a combination of methods is considered a more effective way to learn (Franzoni, Assar, Defude, & Rojas, 2009). The term 'learning styles' has become controversial in recent years, as learners shouldn't necessarily be characterized as having one style or another. However, it is still imperative to provide various sources to heighten engagement, gain new perspectives, and meet the requirements of the time and space the user has for learning.

The design of resources and training programs that are adaptable to user preferences is becoming easier and more effective with the advancement of technologies. It is worth investing time into the initial planning to develop materials in different formats. Resources designed for users to access at their own pace and at a time that suits them, enable far greater learning opportunities. Individuals have differing levels of prior knowledge and varied interests for which static course content doesn't necessarily provide the best outcomes.

> Note – when discussing adaptable learning resources, this is not referring to 'adaptive learning,' which utilizes artificial intelligence and automation to adapt content to the learner as they progress through an instructional pathway. Adaptive learning is discussed further in chapter 6. 'Adaptable learning resources' on the other hand, refers to the provision of options for learners to manually select their own choice of learning material or extension activities.

Initially, the thought of repurposing content in different formats may seem somewhat overwhelming, particularly for smaller companies that are trying to implement adaptable learning resources into their businesses. However, many third-party content providers and software programs such as file, video, and audio converters make repurposing easier. This will result in a more interesting learning pathway that empowers learners to make choices and be more likely to take ownership of their outcomes.

Ultimately, the need for workers to have transferable skills, adaptable attitudes, and access to adaptable and relevant learning resources is significant to their overall development in the workplace. With continuous progression becoming the new norm, adaptability becomes a core competency that allows workers to build upon their skills and knowledge, discover creative solutions and strengthen their resilience. When adaptability is built into learning frameworks, it becomes much easier for individuals, teams, and the overarching business to respond to changing requirements and provides the direction to invigorate companies and their employees for a successful future.

Engagement

Learner engagement can be defined as the active involvement an individual takes in an activity. By comparison, learner motivation represents the driving force behind participation (Appleton, Christenson, Kim, & Reschly, 2006). Needless to say, workplace learning produces favorable results when it is engaging, contextual, and interactive, and the participant is personally motivated to achieve the outcomes. In aiming for full engagement, training activities should be meaningful and connect with the learners' real-life experiences. There are many ways to make learning engaging, including activating multiple senses, providing opportunities to interact with the subject matter, incorporating activities that are considered enjoyable, and learning collaboratively alongside teammates.

To apply higher-order thinking skills, learners should be motivated and engaged with what they are doing. When a learner is genuinely interested and understands how their learning will impact them personally, they are much more likely to be engaged than someone who is motivated only by ticking a checkbox to indicate training completion. Carroll, Lindsey, Chaparro, and Winslow (2019) outline an *Applied Model of Learner Engagement* (Figure 3.1), suggesting that the factors influencing engagement include:

1. The individual. This includes a person's motivation, cognitive ability, interest, personality, self-efficacy, and level of anxiety.
2. The task. The task refers to the perceived challenge, enjoyment, meaningfulness, goals, and feedback that is offered.
3. The environment. The learning environment involves the level of autonomy, safety, and support experienced by the learner.

The outcomes of this type of engagement include the following:

Cognitive outcomes – knowledge and achievement at the macro level and concentration/absorption and loss of awareness at the micro level.

Behavioral outcomes – self-regulation and strategizing at the macro level and performance, involvement, and visual attention at the micro level.

Emotional outcomes – dedication and interest at the macro level and positive affect at the micro level.

Carroll et al. (2019) suggest that the above outline provides measurable indicators for practitioners who wish to assess their learners'

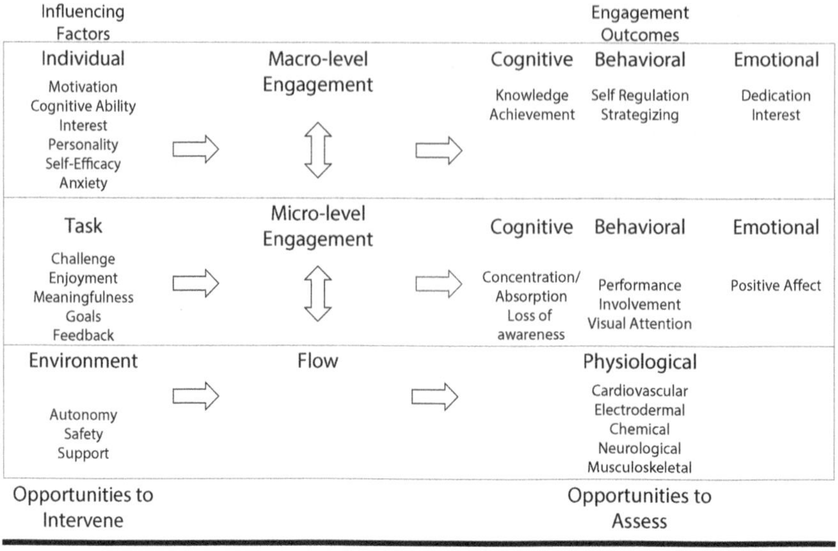

Figure 3.1 Applied model of learner engagement. Adapted from Carroll et al. (2019).

engagement levels. By measuring learner engagement, companies can gain more significant insights into how well their learning programs are performing.

Several strategies can heighten engagement in workplace learning, including a culture of continuous development, encouraging self-directed learning practices in daily life, and providing quality digital learning resources. Keebler, Patzer, Wiltshire, and Fiore (2017) suggest the most appropriate learning resources that promote engagement are immersive technologies such as augmented reality (AR), virtual reality (VR). VR is defined by Jerald (2015) as an artificial environment that is experienced through sensory stimuli provided by a computer, though it is controlled in part by the participant's actions. Whereas AR is defined by Keebler et al. (2017) as the integration of physical reality with digital information overlays, such as visual or auditory information. There are many VR and AR applications on the market that can provide immersive learning experiences within the workplace, and more information about these technologies can be found in Chapter 7.

In general, however, many digital technologies provide greater engagement opportunities through a variety of learning platforms, personalized selection, interesting presentation of content, and collaborative, self-directed experiences. Simply put, Tynjälä (2008) emphasizes that when learners actively participate and immerse themselves in the task, rather than receiving only instructions about how the task is performed, they are invariably more engaged.

For instructional subject matter to be retained and transferred into practice, the learning needs to be engaging. An engaging training program ensures return on investment as the lasting impact of the intended knowledge and skills is realized. With access to various learning mediums, including video, audio, games, guides, AR, VR, e-learning modules, and instructor-led experiences, the engaging learning programs that can be designed could be considered limitless. Learning paths that are interesting, contextual and interactive, provide a meaningful connection to the individual learner and, in turn, improve their learning outcomes.

Flexibility

Flexible learning refers to learning opportunities that can be experienced when, where, and how the user chooses. The learner controls what content they'd like to learn and the time, location, medium, and assessment of the learning experiences. Businesses that provide flexible learning opportunities for their employees allow individuals from various abilities and backgrounds to engage in learning experiences that will suit them, making it much more likely that they will retain and apply what they have learned (Dolasinski & Reynolds, 2020).

Flexibility is not new, and over the past few decades, educators have made it habitual to design differentiated curriculums for learners with special needs (Crawford, 2008; Routley, 2019). These alterations, however, can apply not only to those with special needs but can be extended to suit learners from all demographics, with varying requirements, availability, and preferences (Figure 3.2). As opposed to structured and linear training programs, flexible learning occurs across multiple locations, platforms, and periods. It provides a choice for the typical modern worker whose needs are diverse from those of his peers.

One such example of flexible learning in the workplace is microlearning. Microlearning empowers workers to select their topics of interest and easily digest information in short periods of time. These are particularly useful for those who need to solve specific problems, have lower motivation to undertake training, or need to fill a gap in

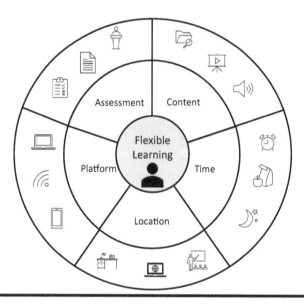

Figure 3.2   Flexible learning in the workplace.

knowledge. Many microlearning platforms offer short, targeted modules, making it easy for workers to start and stop their learning experiences around their other commitments (Dolasinski & Reynolds, 2020).

Another suggestion for flexible learning design can be borrowed from the 'flipped classroom' approach that has become increasingly popular in schools (Berge, 2015). In contrast to the 'instruction and exam' approach, 'flipped' learning basically starts by providing learners with foundational concepts delivered in short, interactive formats, usually online. Learners then have the opportunity to independently engage in activities and research before regrouping and being guided through real-life applications, receiving feedback, and putting the tasks into practice.

Studies carried out by Cook, Watson, and Vegas (2019) examine the effect that flexible learning can have within an organization and report that after a four-year study on preparing higher education students for the workplace, substantial positive gains were made in the learning outcomes of their subjects. As the learners were able to work toward clear objectives at their own pace, they increased confidence and performance.

By utilizing flexible learning approaches such as 'flipped' lessons and microlearning opportunities, individuals can access skills and knowledge that are not necessarily limited by time, location, medium, or type of assessment. The result of such flexible learning has the potential to increase engagement, motivation, and one's personal investment in continuous improvement.

Personalization

Personalized learning is an approach that customizes learning to an individual's prior knowledge, abilities, interests, and objectives. It is usually self-paced and adaptive, including options to alter content once feedback and assessment have been incorporated. As defined by the US Department of Education, Office of Educational Technology (2017), personalized learning

> Refers to instruction in which the pace of learning and the instructional approach are optimized for each learner's needs. Learning objectives, instructional approaches, and instructional content (and its sequencing) may all vary based on learner needs. In addition, learning activities are meaningful and relevant to learners, driven by their interests, and often self-initiated.

This strays from the traditional method of teaching one group of people a standard curriculum and allows for personal traits, preferences, and prior knowledge to influence the design for the individual.

Peng, Ma, and Spector (2019) identify three core elements for personalized learning that are:

1. The learner's individual characteristics
2. The learner's performance
3. The learner's personal development

They also include a fourth element that goes beyond personalization and pushes the practice into personalized adaptive learning, which is *Adaptive Adjustment*. Peng et al. (2019) go on to explain that personalized learning refers to education that is designed, targeted, and paced to meet the needs of the individual learner, while adaptive learning focuses on the technologies and data that are used to evaluate and update instruction as understanding unfolds. The combination of the two is personalized adaptive learning, which is a customized approach to learning that is automatically adapted based on real-time results. (More about adaptive learning can be found in Chapter 6). As discussed by Lin, Zhao, Liu, and Pu (2020), the rise of artificial intelligence and machine learning make it possible to provide such learning programs. By using

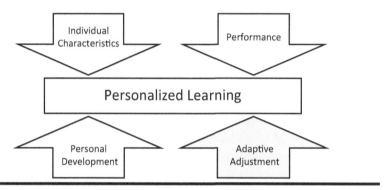

Figure 3.3 Personalized learning in the workplace.

data-driven decision-making intelligence as the core of personalized and adaptive learning frameworks, personalized learning becomes increasingly comprehensive and successful (Figure 3.3). The design of these models is intended to enable differentiated learning methods suited to an individual at a given point in time. Moreover, the mix of diagnostic and formative assessment allows the system to adjust the content delivery in real-time, based on the user's performance and preferences.

As much as we might like to think otherwise, personalized and adaptive learning hasn't been adopted in its full capacity in most workplaces. The potential is there, and it has undoubtedly been adopted in some workplaces; however, it is not yet commonplace for many practitioners to feel comfortable designing fully personalized learning programs for their organization. As a good starting point, many development specialists are using learning management systems (LMS) to deliver basic personalized learning. Examples of some small but impactful features can include:

— Setting personal goals such as completing 100% of a learning path and revising content that wasn't 'passed' by providing the repeat of content in an alternative format.
— Triggering further recommendations for training courses based on the outcomes of completed learning paths.
— Additional buttons for 'more information' allow learners who may not have the background knowledge to discover more about a topic (without all learners having to read through content that they may already be well versed in).

These actions can readily be incorporated into a standard LMS by a system administrator who has a basic understanding of their LMS.

However, artificial intelligence has proven to have far greater abilities to enhance training programs creatively and may be well worth the investment.

Overall, it is fair to say that personalized learning in the workplace allows for greater employee development opportunities and aligns learning goals with business goals more effectively. While there is more potential on the horizon, learning in the workplace can be enhanced today to be more targeted, personalized, and relevant, which can be considered a win-win for both employee and employer.

Accessibility

One imperative for 21st century learning in the workplace is the often-overlooked accessibility to learning programs. The International Organization for Standardization (ISO) defines accessibility as *"the usability of a product, service, environment or facility by people with the widest range of capabilities"* (ISO, 2008), though all too often workplace learning is designed with a one-size-fits-all approach.

It has long been understood that in school education, accessibility can be a real issue for those who are differently abled, have language barriers, and those who may not have access to the tools required, such as digital technology. The latter is often referred to as the 'digital divide' (Dolan, 2016; Power, Musgrove, & Nichols, 2020), separating the 'haves' and 'have nots' into two distinct groups; one that can access advanced hardware and software tools and high-speed internet connectivity, and one that cannot. Therefore, during the COVID-19 pandemic, when millions of individuals were working and learning from home, it would be reasonable to say that the same impact was had on the working population. Those who have access to high-speed internet, quality hardware, and software applications to allow them to perform tasks at a superior level are often outperforming those who have access to poor quality equipment, lack of software licenses, and other resources.

Evaluating accessible learning in the workplace is an ongoing process that cycles through three stages:

(1) Identifying barriers to access.
(2) Investigating ways to resolve these barriers.
(3) Incorporating accessible resources and opportunities into learning programs.

Such accessible resources include digital tools that can be accessed wherever learning occurs (such as at home or in the library) as well as assistive technologies (AT) for those who may have special needs such as sight or hearing impairment (Akpan & Beard, 2013), or limited dexterity.

According to Parette (1997), the use of AT for learning is concerned with two categories:

1. 'AT devices' which are used to increase or improve access to training opportunities and can be configured to the needs of the individual. These can include screen readers, mobility aids, extendable reaching devices, and so on.
2. 'AT services' which involve training groups and individuals on how to use the abovementioned devices.

Note – when planning workplace learning programs, it is important to include training on AT devices for users who rely on these technologies and the people who consequently interact with them.

Taking into account simple functions such as text readability, navigation of material, and the appropriate level of language for the intended audience are good starting points for the overall design of accessible learning programs. Despite the fact that, according to Rogers-Shaw, Carr-Chellman, and Choi (2018), there is no universally designed concept of how adults should access learning resources in the workplace, Universal Design Learning (UDL) gives us a broad conceptual framework in which we can accommodate the diversity of learners in any workplace (Figure 3.4).

UDL provides equal opportunity for all learners. It is a framework that conceptualizes knowledge through the focus on the learner and emphasizes collaboration and accessibility (Rogers-Shaw et al., 2018). The three guiding principles of UDL are:

1. Providing multiple ways to represent content.
2. Allowing choices of assessment methods.
3. Providing various ways to motivate people to learn.

Rogers-Shaw et al. (2018) explain that although UDL was designed with the needs of disabled learners in mind, it can be successfully

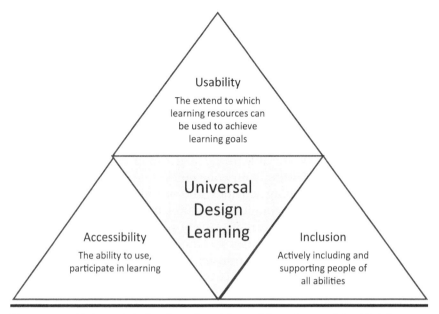

Figure 3.4   Universal design learning. Adapted from Burgstahler (2009).

implemented into learning frameworks for everyone. They also point out that there are significant differences in what motivates and engages an individual, stemming from their background knowledge, culture, and personal situation. Therefore, recognizing that the learner constructs knowledge within the paradigm of their own personal view, it becomes even more critical that they can choose how they learn (Rogers-Shaw et al., 2018).

Accessibility options are ideally built into all designs because even if there are no trainees who have identified as being differently abled, there is always staff turnover, changes to individual's health, and the probability that there are people who will not disclose that they experience challenges. Studies carried out by Moorefield-Lang, Copeland, and Haynes (2016) revealed that 80 percent of online instructors admitted they did not consider accessibility when designing their courses. They also claim that as many as one in seven people experience some sort of learning disability, making this a mismatch that could lead to training program failure, purely because the intended users cannot properly access or engage with the curriculum.

Social Learning

Social learning is an active and engaging process that allows for meaningful connections to be made between prior knowledge, new information, and the broader understanding of the group. Environmental and cognitive factors interact to influence learning and behavior, and meaning can be made through observation, mediation, and evaluation.

Social learning has always occurred in the workplace, though it is gaining increasing attention in recent times. Bingham and Conner (2010) describe 'new' social learning as learning from others in informal ways such as chatting with colleagues, mingling at conferences, conversing during training activities, and of course, interacting online. They emphasize how technology amplifies the social aspect of learning and that social media can effectively support social learning.

New social learning reframes social media from being a marketing tool to one that facilitates the transfer of information and knowledge between people. Provided this is done responsibly, it can result in a more informed community on a variety of topics, width broader perspectives, and the ability to make improved decisions by verifying information with others (Bingham & Conner, 2010). It is worth noting that traditional training provides solutions to problems that have already been solved, whereas collaborating on new ideas can address challenges that haven't yet been overcome. Social media can provide a platform to share such ideas and resources and bring together groups interested in similar topics.

It is human nature for people to learn from one another and collaborate on their ideas, problems, and interests. They absorb information and imitate actions, and when done more consciously, the learner can evaluate the validity and effectiveness of new ideas, skills, knowledge, and information before assimilating them into their own understanding. The very nature of organizations is that they are social communities that tend to learn from those in their networks, such as their customers, partners, suppliers, and competitors (Ratten & Suseno, 2006).

As human capital theory focuses on a company's investment in their human resources by developing their skills and knowledge (Ratten & Suseno, 2006), the social capital theory focuses on the effectiveness of social groups with shared values and understandings and a collective sense of identity. Social capital can be leveraged in the workplace by strengthening social relationships, trust, and cooperation among groups. Strong social networks can demonstrate the creation of intellectual qualities, work well in cross-functional teams, and increase intercompany learning (Ratten & Suseno, 2006). When discussing social learning, it is essential to consider the increasing shift to online learning instruction. The strength and impact of social interactions are usually influenced by the instructor's facilitation or lack thereof. The instructor's role usually unfolds in three stages, the first being that of the guide, facilitating discussions during a time where most learners prefer to observe than participate. During the second stage, instructors tend to foster conversations and interaction by prompting participants and providing collaborative activities. Throughout the third phase, the instructor transfers to being more of an observer and allows them to interact freely with their peers (Ouyang & Scharber, 2017).

After reviewing the literature on the subject, Ouyang and Scharber (2017) observed claims that online learning tended to yield a reduced sense of connectedness and participation. However, after conducting their own studies, they concluded that the instructor's role could enable strong networks among the group and coach them to work well together. They say that the instructor should take on the role of the facilitator, forming a more symmetrical relationship with their trainees, and use a balance of participation in discussions with a gradual relinquishment of authority as the participants progress. Either way, social learning is here to stay, and it can be a powerful tool for developing skills and encouraging peers to engage in active learning. Companies that foster social learning are more likely to leverage their workers' potential and create a positive culture of continuous development throughout the workplace.

Meaningful Assessment

Few educators would argue the importance of assessment as part of an effective learning program (Figure 3.5). Assessment is the key to determining worker competencies, future training objectives, and contributing to the data that reveals how training programs perform. Without effective assessment, programs lack accurate information to guide the learning requirements and incremental improvements over time. However, assessment should never be just for the sake of it, and instead, should be meaningful. In order to do this, the objective must first be considered; what knowledge or skills should the learner obtain, and how can this be demonstrated? It is this desired

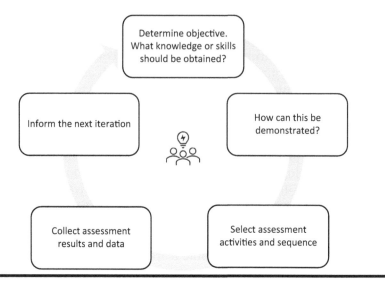

Figure 3.5   Meaningful assessment in the workplace.

demonstration that should drive the choice and sequence of assessment activities, and lead to the collection of data that can inform the next step.

There are several types of assessment, and here we consider the three main classifications, diagnostic, formative, and summative assessments, and their characteristics.

Diagnostic assessment is usually the initial phase in the learning cycle and is described as the assessment that is used to identify a learner's requirements and abilities, as well as their readiness to acquire the knowledge and skills that are outlined in the subsequent training (Ontario Ministry of Education, 2013). A diagnostic assessment will most commonly occur before the final design of a training program. It can be used as a critical metric for setting the appropriate content and objectives.

Formative assessment is defined as *"a planned process in which assessment-elicited evidence of students' status is used by [instructors] to adjust their ongoing instructional procedures or by [learners] to adjust their current learning tactics"* (Popham, 2008). This type of assessment carries out small, frequent assessments throughout learning, during the process of instruction (Clark, 2011), often assessing narrow components of proficiency and using assessment data to assist with incremental learning (Newton, 2007).

Whereas summative assessment aims to measure and quantify learning achievement at a particular time based on pre-set criteria or standards. The assessment results become the source of making inferences about the learner's competence (Ahmad, 2020). This assessment type is usually completed after the information has been transferred (at the end of a module or course), often to gain formal recognition or certification. Usually, it focuses on the broader abilities expected to be attained from the training (Newton, 2007).

Assessment design is best when it is not limited to one form of measurement and should look at several information sources and data points to gain a holistic picture. A variety of assessment tasks can be measured differently and can include observation, demonstration, interviews, quizzes, self-assessment, exams, simulations, and hands-on workplace tasks. When designing a well-rounded approach to assessment, the practice could be enhanced in three ways.

1. Aim to gather data that will assist the learner and the instructor.

Assessment data assists decision-making around student attainment, diagnosing skill gaps, and providing quality, targeted feedback or additional learning opportunities. However, it also has a significant place in evaluating course programs and informs decisions about instruction materials, learning experiences, and technologies, and can also help administrators document their course outcomes for accreditation purposes (Martin, Ritzhaupt, Kumar, & Budhrani, 2019).

2. Provide quality corrective instruction where required.

Optimal assessment practice is continuous, objective, corrective, and provides timely feedback and instruction. By providing corrective instruction in a timely manner, the learner can reflect on their performance, reinforce their understandings of what they have achieved, and take steps to bridge any gaps in knowledge.

3. Provide reassessment opportunities where appropriate.

Concluding that an individual or group has not 'passed' an assessment should not be the end of the exercise. The areas in which they were lacking can often be reabsorbed by taking a different approach to delivering the content. Once a learner has had time to acquire the skill or knowledge via the new approach, a reassessment is required to assess whether the competency has since been attained.

Continuous assessment provides regular feedback to workers and reinforces the efficacy of training programs. Assessment needs to be meaningful and not just incorporated for the purpose of exam regurgitation (Nguyen, 2020). Performance metrics inform which individuals are thriving and those who are struggling. These measurements – emphasizing the process rather than the outcome – are an ideal starting point as they reveal details about minor performance issues that may otherwise go unnoticed. Whether the assessment is diagnostic, formative, or summative, there is a place for assessment to be embedded and evaluated in all workplace learning initiatives.

As a learning imperative for the 21st century workplace, assessment is a vast topic that is deserved of its own books (of which they are many and varied) and is barely touched on here. However, what is important to note is that assessment is a driving force for workplace training, and providing a one-stop summative assessment at the end of a training session will no longer suffice. Assessments should be well-thought-out and varied, collecting purposeful data points to inform the learner's future development plans and the training programs across the organization.

Relevance

From the perspectives of both the organization and the individual, there is no point in carrying out training if it doesn't bear relevance to the workplace activity. Relevance is defined in the Oxford Dictionary as *"closely connected with the subject you are discussing or the situation you are in"* (Waite & Soanes, 2007), and if the intended education is not closely aligned with what the learner needs to achieve to perform their job, it fails to be relevant.

When implementing learning programs into an organization, it should be clear that the purpose is for workers to apply the newly acquired knowledge and skills to their day-to-day workplace activity. In this section, we look at three aspects of relevance for workplace learning.

1. Application of new skills in the workplace.
2. Alignment of organizational strategy and individual goals.
3. Recognition of professional skills and development.

Application of New Skills in the Workplace

For workplace training to be effective, workers need to realize the benefits. By understanding that the newly acquired skills and knowledge will make their day-to-day job more manageable, more productive, less risky, or more satisfying, their potential buy-in and participation is usually heightened. The training should have relevance to them as individuals and relevance to their role within the company.

The OECD (2017) points out that workers, companies, and society all benefit from people putting their skills to better use and can be positively associated with being satisfied and productive at work. For the learning and development professional, this means looking for evidence that the intended skillsets can be applied to impact business outcomes. It also means that after the training has occurred, that follow-ups take place, which evaluate how learners feel they have improved their performance, any problems they needed to overcome, and how many individuals may have reverted to old ways of working. These insights inform improved training programs for the future.

Alignment of Organizational Strategy and Individual Goals

Learning opportunities that align organizational strategy and individual goals resonate with the employee and the employer alike. For ongoing learning experiences to be relevant, there should be a clear articulation of how the curriculum links to company strategy, the worker's goals, and the overall bigger picture. When alignment occurs, there is an improved understanding of how skills and knowledge are acquired and used. Learning doesn't occur within a silo, starting at the beginning of the course and finishing at the end. There are critical stages of learning that occur before, during, and most importantly after, allowing the individual to grasp a true comprehension of the new information and how it links to the broader outcomes.

Recognition of Professional Skills and Development

The recognition of skills and knowledge in the workplace makes the relevance of such accomplishments evident. When knowledge and skill acquisition are brought into focus, allowing workers to take pride in their achievements, it clearly demonstrates that the learning has relevance to their role within the organization.

Official skill recognition is often asserted at a state or national level, where certifications and qualifications are awarded once a learner has completed the coursework and passed the necessary assessments. However, recognizing skills that have been acquired in the workplace through semi-formal training or informal learning can be recognized in other ways. For example, these competencies can be measured as key performance indicators against agreed standards for a particular role or by encouraging self-reflection. (There is a cross-organizational record that is growing in popularity for its ability to record and validate an individual's skills and knowledge called the *Comprehensive Learner Record*. More can be read about this in Chapter 8).

Therefore, by designing learning opportunities that allow individuals to (1) apply newly acquired information to their job, (2) align learning to organizational strategy and individual goals, and (3) receive recognition for what has been learned, this can result in relevant and optimal learning opportunities across the workplace.

Conclusion

Over the past two decades, organizations have undergone significant and lasting change due to the advancements of digital technology. The rate of this change was accelerated due to the COVID-19 pandemic, which forced employers to undertake steep learning curves and reconsider how their businesses operate. To remain competitive in this changing world, reskilling, upskilling, and rethinking ways of working have become essential. Outlined above are eight of the imperatives that should underpin learning as we move into the future.

These eight learning imperatives (adaptability, engagement, flexibility, personalization, accessibility, social learning, meaningful assessment, and relevance) can be considered the foundation for modern learning design and development. They form the basis for sound learning frameworks in the workplace and allow for the delivery of quality learning outcomes in the digital age.

Critical Thinking Questions

1   Which of these learning imperatives is the most essential, and does this vary depending on the technology platform used to enable instruction?

2 Because we are living in a state of constant flux, are there other learning imperatives that will be more relevant in the future, or ideas that used to be essential but are no longer relevant?

3 How often do technology-enhanced training programs exhibit these eight elements?

4 Personalization for learning will perhaps be the quality that evolves most significantly. In what ways will this evolve, and what will it mean for lifelong learning?

5 Is Universal Design Learning still the most appropriate framework for accessibility today? Are there elements of UDL that will need to alter/expand as technology evolves?

References

Ahmad, Z. (2020). Summative assessment, test scores, and text quality: A study of cohesion as an unspecified descriptor in the assessment scale. *European Journal of Educational Research*, *9*(2), 523–535. DOI: 10.12973/EU-jer.9.2.523

Akpan, J. P., & Beard, L. A. (2013). Overview of assistive technology possibilities for teachers to enhance academic outcomes of all students. *Universal Journal of Educational Research*, *1*(2), 113–118. DOI: 10.13189/ujer.2013.101211

Appleton, J. J., Christenson, S. L., Kim, D., & Reschly, A. L. (2006). Measuring cognitive and psychological engagement: Validation of the Student Engagement Instrument. *Journal of School Psychology*, *44*(5), 427–445. DOI: 10.13189/ujer.2013.010211

Berge, Z. (2015). Flipped learning in the workplace. *Journal of Workplace Learning*, *27*(2), 162–172. DOI:10.1108/JWL-06-2014-0044

Bingham, T., & Conner, M. (2010). *The new social learning: A guide to transforming organizations through social media*. California: Association for Talent Development & Berrett-Koehler.

Brown, K. (2017). Introduction and overview: Now more than ever. In K. Brown (Ed.), *The Cambridge handbook of workplace training and employee development* (Cambridge Handbooks in Psychology, pp. 1–8). Cambridge University Press. DOI:10.1017/9781316091067.003

Burgstahler, S. (2009). Universal Design in Education: Principles and Applications. *DO-IT*. Retrieved April 20 2021 from https://www.washington.edu/doit/sites/default/files/atoms/files/UDE-Principles-and-Applications.pdf

Calarco, A., & Gurvis, J. (2006). *Adaptability: Responding effectively to change*. North Carolina: Center for Creative Leadership.

Carroll, M., Lindsey, S., Chaparro, M., & Winslow, B. (2019). An applied model of learner engagement and strategies for increasing learner engagement in the modern educational environment. *Interactive Learning Environments*, 1–15. doi:10.1080/10494820.2019.1636083

Clark, I. (2011). Formative assessment: Policy, perspectives and practice. *Florida Journal of Educational Administration & Policy*, 4(2), 158–180.

Clark, J. M., & Paivio, A. (1991). Dual coding theory and education. *Educational Psychology Review*, 3(3), 149-210. DOI:10.1107/BF01320076

Cook. S., Watson. D., & Vegas. D. (2019). Solving the quantitative skills gap: A flexible learning call to arms! *Higher Education Pedagogies*, 4(1), 17-31. DOI:10.1080/23752696.2018.1564880

Crawford, G. B. (2008). *Differentiation for the adolescent learner: Accommodating brain development, language, literacy, and special needs.* California: Corwin.

Dolan, J. E. (2016). Splicing the divide: A review of research on the evolving digital divide among K–12 students. *Journal of Research on Technology in Education*, 48(1), 16-37. DOI:10.1080/15391523.2015.1103147

Dolasinski, M. J., & Reynolds, J. (2020). Microlearning: A new learning model. *Journal of Hospitality and Tourism Research*, 44(3), 551–561. DOI:10.1177/1096348020901579

Franzoni, A. L., Assar, S., Defude, B., & Rojas, J. (2009). Student learning styles adaptation method based on teaching strategies and electronic media. *Educational Technology & Society*, 12(4), 15–29. DOI: 10.12691/education-6-11-7

ISO. (2008). 9241-171-Ergonomics of human-system interaction–Guidance on software accessibility. *ISO, Ed.*

Jerald, J. (2015) *The VR book: Human-centered design for virtual reality.* California: Morgan & Claypool Publishers and ACM Books.

Keebler, J., Patzer, B., Wiltshire, T., & Fiore, S. (2017). Augmented reality systems in training. In K. Brown (Ed.), *The Cambridge handbook of workplace training and employee development* (Cambridge Handbooks in Psychology, pp. 278–292). Cambridge University Press. DOI:10.1017/9781316091067.014

Lin, J., Zhao, Y., Liu, C., & Pu, H. (2020). Personalized learning service based on big data for education. In *2020 IEEE 2nd International Conference on Computer Science and Educational Informatization (CSEI)* (pp. 235–238). Xinxiang, China: IEEE.

Macgregor, G. (2005). The nature of information in the twenty-first century: Conundrums for the informatics community? *Library Review*, 51(1), 10–23. DOI:10.1108/00242530510574129

Martin, F., Ritzhaupt, A., Kumar, S., & Budhrani, K. (2019). Award-winning faculty online teaching practices: Course design, assessment and evaluation, and facilitation. *The Internet and Higher Education*, 42, 34–43. DOI:10.1016/j.iheduc.2019.04.00

Merriam-Webster, D. (2020). Adaptability. *Merriam-webster.com diction-ary.* Retrieved from https://www.merriam-webster.com/dictionary/adaptability

Moorefield-Lang, H., Copeland, C. A., & Haynes, A. (2016). Accessing abili-ties: Creating innovative accessible online learning environments and putting quality into practice. *Education for Information, 32*(1), 27–33. DOI:10.3233/EFI-150966

Newton, P. E. (2007). Clarifying the purposes of educational assessment. *Assessment in Education: Principles, Policy & Practice, 14*(2), 149–170. DOI:10.1080/09695940701458321

Nguyen, J. (2020). *A human's guide to the future.* Pan McMillan: Australia.

Office of Educational Technology, US Department of Education. (2017). Reimagining the role of technology in education: 2017 National Education Technology Plan update. Retrieved from https://tech.ed.gov/files/2017/01/NETP17.pdf

Ontario Ministry of Education. (2013). Police/program memorandum 155, diagnostic assessment in support of student learning. Retrieved July 26, 2020, from http://www.edu.gov.on.ca/extra/eng/ppm/ppm155.pdf

Organisation for Economic Co-operation and Development. (2017). *Better use of skills in the workplace: Why it matters for productivity and local jobs.* Paris: OECD.

Ouyang, F., & Scharber, C., (2017). The influences of an experienced instruc-tor's discussion design and facilitation on an online learning community development: a social network analysis study. *The Internet and Higher Education, 35*(1), 34–47. DOI:10.1016/j.iheduc.2017.07.002

Parette, H. (1997). Assistive technology devices and services. *Education and Training in Mental Retardation and Developmental Disabilities, 32*(4), 267–280. Retrieved February 17, 2021, from http://www.jstor.org/stable/23879197

Peng, H., Ma, S., & Spector, J. M. (2019). Personalized adaptive learning: An emerging pedagogical approach enabled by a smart learning environment. *Smart Learning Environments, 6*(1), 9. DOI:10.1186/s40561-019-0089-y

Popham, W. J. (2008). *Transformative assessment.* Virginia: Association for Supervision and Curriculum Development.

Power, J. R., Musgrove, A. T., & Nichols, B. H. (2020). Teachers bridging the digital divide in rural schools with 1:1 computing. *Rural Educator, 41*(1), 61–76. DOI:10.35608/ruraled.v41i1.57

Ratten, V., & Suseno, Y. (2006). Knowledge development, social capital and alliance learning. *International Journal of Education Management, 20*(1), 60–72. DOI:10.1108/0951354061063959

Rogers-Shaw, C., Carr-Chellman, D. J., & Choi, J. (2018). Universal design for learning: Guidelines for accessible online instruction. *Adult Learning, 29*(1), 20–31. doi:10.1177/1045159517735530

Routley, C. (2019). *Special learners in school: Understanding essential concepts*. New York: Routledge.

Tynjälä, P. (2008). Perspectives into learning at the workplace. *Educational Research Review, 3*(2), 130–154. DOI:10.1016/j.edurev.2007.12.001

Waite, M., & Soanes, C. (2007). *Oxford dictionary and thesaurus* (2nd ed.). London: Oxford University Press.

Chapter 4

The Digital Future of the Workplace: Three Possible Scenarios

While a paradigm can explain new phenomena, it will endure. Once it can no longer assimilate changes into its fundamental construct, it will shift. We are now witnessing perhaps the most significant paradigm shift the fields of organizational learning and professional development have yet seen.

The digital revolution is the foundation on which these changes occur, disseminating modern technologies that rapidly impact how we learn and work and thrusting us into an environment of continuous change. The rise of digital technology has resulted in a profound transformation of the organizational landscape. The rate of digital advancement is accelerating across the globe, and the pace of change blurs the boundaries between the physical and digital worlds. As disruptive technologies redefine traditional industry sectors and the roles workers play, the advancement of artificial intelligence (A.I.), robotics, and automation alters the organizational setting. It highlights the importance of human-centric consideration and agile practices.

Organizational learning has been identified by Belinski, Peixe, Frederico, and Garza-Reyes (2020) as the most crucial subject in this new context as employers and employees alike adapt to these evolving technologies. The reason for this is because when organizations

DOI: 10.1201/9781003149132-5

and individuals commit themselves to ongoing learning practices, they increase their ability to react quickly to fast-changing market conditions. When faced with challenges, they can apply creative solutions and are more likely to recognize and leverage new opportunities.

In this chapter, three future workplace scenarios are considered in the context of our evolving digital landscape and their predicted effects on organizational and personal learning. These scenarios are (1) the human-centered design approach, (2) integrated artificial intelligence, and (3) the agile adaptors. The most likely future will comprise aspects of all three scenarios varying in degree across different industries and demographics. The rate at which technology develops, the workplace adapts, and organizational learning evolves are likely to shape these future outcomes.

Scenario #1: The Human-Centered Design Approach

Human-centered design (HCD) is a collaborative approach that starts with the end user's needs in mind and ends with a product, service, or experience that meets their requirements. It focuses on working with the people it intends to serve, generating creative ideas, building prototypes, and incorporating user feedback into the design. Originally developed to improve products and services for customers, HCD is now used to design workplace experiences, and in some instances, organizational and professional learning programs. It makes sense that an HCD within the workplace leads to workers feeling more empowered to make decisions and more productive in their work.

In a 2018 report on the Workforce of the Future, Price Waterhouse Coopers (PWC) defined a human-centric scenario they called the 'Yellow World' (PWC, 2018) (Figure 4.1). This scenario focuses on workplace flexibility, autonomy, and fulfillment and reshapes employee/employer relationships based on the HCD approach. PWC describes this future workplace as one where workers and companies seek positive meaning and relevance in their outputs and achievements. Technology breaks down barriers by providing access to opportunities from crowdfunding ideas to working-from-home arrangements. PWC envisages workers as having less attachment to single employers and predicts that new worker guilds will act as associations who train, support, and connect workers and oversee their working arrangements in the traditional way that employers have done. As a result, it is expected that individual loyalties will be

People strategy	What does the workforce look like?	Organizational challenges
• Business leaders are responsible for people direction and management. • HR rarely exists as a separate function, as organizations rely on outsourced services, specialist suppliers and automation for people processes. • Guilds support workers to build skills and experience by providing training and career development support alongside other help and advice. • Digital platforms create mobility and help match workers with employers and skills and attributes with demand. • Performance is above delivering an organizational goal but also about employee's behaviors and societal impact.	• Like-minded workers gravitate towards each other, aided by technology platforms. • Individuals come together to collaborate on projects or to deliver on an idea. • Guilds help workers create scale when needed, remain current and build trust in their services. • Guilds provide members with a strong sense of identity – individuals see themselves as members of their profession, identifying with each other because of their particular skills set, interests and goals. • Work is often a fluid concept and a regimented 9 to 5, Monday to Friday working week is rare. Borders between home and work are blurred.	• Brand and good ethical record is essential in the Yellow World. The risk of brand damage from rogue workers must be actively managed. • Organizations are judged on trust and fairness; organizational purpose must be clearly articulated and demonstrated. • Ethical and transparent supply chain management is critical and penalties apply for non-compliance. • In the Yellow World, relationships with governments and NGO's are vital and need to be closely managed.

Figure 4.1 Characteristics of the 'Yellow World'. Adapted from Price, Waterhouse, Coopers (2018).

strongest among groups of people working in the same fields or who have similar skill sets, rather than to any particular company. While individuals are responsible for their own lifelong learning, they will turn to guilds and other professional organizations to provide learning programs and develop their skills and attributes. Online personas will be a feature, and worker's performance will be measured not only by reaching professional goals but by personal behaviors and societal impact (PWC, 2018).

Considering the HCD of this approach and that professional development would be primarily self-directed, applying a learning framework such as the Reference Human-Centric Architecture Model (RHCAM) (Figure 4.2) helps identify purposeful learning opportunities (Flores, Xu, & Lu, 2020). RHCAM distinguishes the competency layers of self-awareness, cognitive, soft, and social skills, hard and technical skills, and digital skills. Understanding these competencies' breakdown is useful as the demand for skills skyrockets. Most existing education and training initiatives are not actually competency-based but are instead subject-based and purely hard skill-driven (Flores et al., 2020).

Flores et al. (2020) suggest that this architecture can be used to tailor training content according to personal requirements. There are two main ways to do this; the first is to apply it to problems as

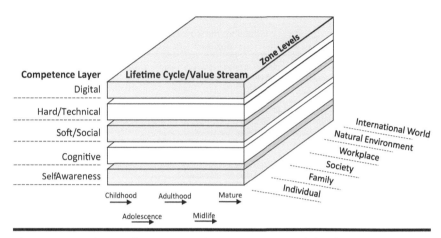

Figure 4.2   Reference human-centric architecture model. Adapted from Flores et al. (2020).

they arise (e.g., transitioning workers to work-from-home arrangements for the first time). The second is to use it as a framework for complete, HCD personalized training programs (e.g., learning how to adapt to a newly implemented client management system). By leveraging multiple competency levels, holistic and lasting development is more likely to occur.

However, there is no standard 'starting point,' and the need for all workers of the future human-centric workplace to develop their competencies in line with this approach would be impacted by age, attitude, ability, and past experience (Romero, Noran, Stahre, Bernus, & Fast-Berglund, 2015). This further reinforces the need for learning to be designed in a human-centered way rather than a one-size-fits-all or assumption-based approach.

PWC's Yellow World is a place where individuals can make their requirements known and take control of their own professional learning journey (PWC, 2018). Unlike the historic hierarchical structure where senior management determined what was suitable for every worker and how they would progress and operate, in this world, workers are empowered with human responses to human challenges.

Developing Learning Programs Using HCD

HCD for learning is a creative approach to designing and refining solutions. It involves cultivating deep empathy with the intended

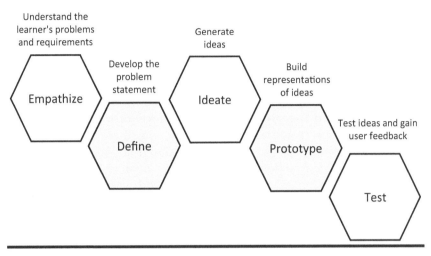

Figure 4.3   Learning programs using human-centered design.

users and experiments with ideas, generates prototypes, and uses continuous feedback and informative data to improve the solution.

Design thinking is an innovative process that can form the foundation of contextualized learning solutions and continually improve learning and development offerings across the organization (Figure 4.3). HCD for training uses fast-paced prototyping techniques to address employee needs and develop the learning and performance solutions that will support them. The following stages can be used, although they are not linear, but intertwined and developed concurrently.

Empathize

As with most learning and development approaches, they begin with analyzing the current state and delving into the learner's problems and requirements. During this stage, activities such as training needs analysis, task analysis, and interviews are conducted. However, with design thinking, this stage goes further into uncovering the deeper, fundamental needs of the learner.

Assumptions are put aside, and the end user's requirements are aimed to be fully understood and within the context of their working environment, previous knowledge, and requirements of their roles and the broader organization. This strategic planning activity includes all stakeholders relevant to the program's development and creates a shared vision (Maguire, 2001) for how the learning program can support the business objectives.

Define

The next stage in the process is the synthesis of ideas. During this stage, information from the previous stage is gathered and analyzed. Observations and ideas are synthesized to define core problems and develop a 'problem statement' in a human-centered manner. Ideas are created quickly, and the results are shared with the focus group to provide feedback. Problem statements are usually worded in such a way that it focuses on the learner rather than the trainer or the company. For example, replacing a statement such as 'digital literacy amongst workers needs to increase by 20% across the organization,' with a statement such as 'workers who are enabled to raise their digital literacy skills by 20% can feel more confident and capable when working with technology in the workplace.'

Furthermore, this stage establishes features and elements that allow the problem to be solved and lead into the ideation phase. This is achieved by posing questions that can inform solutions such as 'how can digital learning activities lead to the benefits realization of using technology in the workplace?' or 'which digital skillsets can workers learn and incorporate into their daily lives to make their tasks easier?'

Ideation

The third stage of the process is ideation, during which time the previous information is evaluated and ideas are generated (Knapp, 2016). By using the problem statements, the team can start to generate many ideas and look for alternative ways to solve problems. There are many ideation techniques, including some that Maguire (2001) lists as:

— Brainstorming (curating a list of ideas spontaneously contributed by stakeholders.)
— Parallel design (stakeholders create their own designs from the requirements. Individuals work independently and, when finished, share their concepts with the group.)

— Storyboarding (a visual organizer consisting of words and images displayed in sequence to represent the desired outcomes.)
— Affinity diagram (a visual tool used to organize a large number of ideas and their relationships, usually taken from the output of a brainstorming session.)

The goal is to generate many ideas using creativity and innovation to think 'outside the box,' and by expanding the scope of solution modeling, the team can find more creative and suitable solutions to the problem statements.

Prototype

Prototypes make design ideas tangible, increase the quality of user feedback, and the evaluation is used to inform the next iteration of development. This allows for a diverse number of ideas to be 'tested' and users to experiment with the end product while avoiding the focus on perfection, as that slows the process down (Meier & Miller, 2016). This prototyping process repeats as new ideas and features are integrated into the design.

In the context of workplace learning initiatives, particularly when it comes to sophisticated techniques such as personalization or adaptive learning, the prototype allows real learners to engage with lessons, courses, and learning pathways. Often, once experiencing the program in a 'hands-on' manner, the user may identify that the outcomes were not as expected, leading to revaluation and continuous improvement. Rapid prototyping allows the end user to experience the solution at an early stage and uncover these problems, meaning that the cost of failure is low (Meier & Miller, 2016). In turn, this allows learning and development professionals to discover issues early in development, resulting in far less rework than traditional approaches.

Testing

Testing should be carried out early and often so the results can inform the subsequent stages of design and development. It's the chance to have the prototypes utilized by real users who will experience the program as it evolves (Knapp, 2016). During the testing phase, it is possible to realize that the problem statements may not have been framed correctly, and this would lead the design back to earlier stages of the process.

Experiencing the program first-hand, users can provide suggestions or reveal any anomalies that may otherwise have gone unnoticed. It is also common during testing that users will uncover needs and requirements that did not come up in the initial planning phase and can be incorporated for further consideration. As testing unfolds, alterations may be made as the design team gain a deeper understanding of the end user's problems and requirements.

Overall, the HCD approach takes the whole person into account, acknowledging the variety of competencies, and considering prior experience, interests, and aspirations, so a powerful and positive impact can be made (PWC, 2018). Future directions for the HCD approach will be entrenched in technology and its ongoing advancements. Learners will assist in the ongoing evaluation of their own learning pathways, and the needs of both the worker and the company will be recognized and met.

Scenario #2: Integrated Artificial Intelligence

The workplace that features integrated A.I. is a much-discussed and inevitable future that assimilates automation and robotics into the organizational landscape. For the purposes of this discussion, this scenario is not intended to be an A.I.-dominated landscape but instead an earlier stage prediction where machines and humans work together harmoniously.

A.I. makes it possible for machines to learn from the tasks they are programmed to complete and perform many human-like activities. By processing large amounts of data and recognizing and responding to patterns, A.I. can automate tasks with precision and speed, meaning that they can often 'outperform' their human counterparts who may make mistakes and take longer times to complete such tasks (Harari, 2019; Kelly, 2017; Nguyen, 2020). Automation is becoming incredibly popular as a time and cost-saving investment in many industries, as activities can be carried out at scale by accurate and reliable machines.

However, the perception of A.I. and robotics having human-like qualities, as pointed out by Southgate (2020), is commonly overestimated. While human-style robots are regularly depicted in science fiction, the reality is that most A.I. is designed to perform narrowly focused tasks and are unable to exhibit forms of intelligence that are outside of their purpose (Kelly, 2017). Nevertheless, many people are legitimately concerned about the future of their work being taken over by intelligent robots.

It is important to note that people are more than just task performers. By outsourcing many of their existing repetitive and mundane duties, workers will be freed up to perform new tasks involving higher-level skills such as problem-solving, creativity, and evaluation (Harari, 2019). Some of the initial fears people expressed around robots overtaking human jobs have subsided with the understanding that machines may assist them rather than steal from them (Kelly, 2017). Consider the fact that various forms of A.I. have been around for decades and have (for the most part) made a positive impact on people's working lives. Repetitive tasks like sending out recurring meeting invites (now done through email), searching for the information needed for your next meeting (now typed into search engines), or asking questions to an online chatbot rather than listening to hold music on the telephone for half an hour have been welcome advancements. Therefore, in many ways, integrating A.I. with human workers allows for increased productivity. Suppose this is combined with a culture of motivated, continuous learning. In that case, purposeful and targeted training will enable workers to develop skills and adapt to working with A.I. rather than being quashed by it.

Learning pathways in this future scenario will be twofold:

1. Learning how to use and work with A.I. integrations, and
2. Learning how to perform new tasks that have been opened up as a result of A.I.

Ongoing and regular training play an increasingly important role within any digital change framework, as it keeps workers abreast of technological advancements at regular intervals. A.I. integrated organizations of the future are expected to allow time in lieu or education leave if training needs to be completed outside of work hours (many countries, particularly in Europe, are already firmly embracing this). However, most training will be embedded into daily working life.

A.I. technologies that are developed to aid learning are appearing at a rapid rate. The 20th International Conference for Artificial Intelligence in Education held in Chicago in 2019 presented a significant number of A.I. progressions for organizational learning

(Isotani et al., 2019), acknowledging that there is tremendous potential to deliver more in-depth and more meaningful learning from digital experiences. Some of the exhibited intelligence included performance predictions, automated summarization of large amounts of text, game-based learning environments, and mind-wandering reduction through intelligent monitoring systems (Isotani et al., 2019). These are just a handful of innovative A.I. technologies that will help advance learning programs for the future.

Developing Learning Programs Using A.I.

The uses for A.I. in the workplace are growing exponentially, and with the appropriate setup, the opportunities are almost limitless. Following are some examples of common practices in learning and development that can be enhanced and streamlined through A.I.

Training Needs Analysis

A.I. can be leveraged to identify training needs and link learning-related metrics to business outcomes. By combining adaptive testing with machine learning, statistical models can be developed that align competencies to requirements. Algorithms can be adjusted to put more weight on complex skills rather than simple yes/no style answers that yield equal scoring. By understanding the skills and knowledge that a worker has prior to training, programs can eliminate modules that will not provide good use of their time if the worker has already mastered the content.

Content Development

There are increasing options within content development software such as Adobe Captivate and Articulate Storyline to integrate A.I. using APIs, plug-ins, and other digital tools. This type of A.I. can suggest the most appropriate text arrangements, graphics, templates, and storyboards based on what it deems to be the most effective elements for a particular instance, leading to improved content production.

Another example of A.I.-influenced content development is the use of intelligent chatbots. These chatbots are programmed to interpret keywords provided to them by the user and, consequently, offer pre-set answers. By combining historical information along with well-defined rules, the program can begin to understand user preferences, the context of conversations and solve user problems.

Adaptive Content

Intelligent adaptive systems can enable differentiated learning experiences at a personalized level (Lin, Zhao, Liu, & Pu, 2020). Because A.I. can generate an understanding of learner needs through sources such as data analytics, it can make suggestions for additional training or ways in which existing training programs can be enhanced for improved applicability.

Yuan (2019) describes adaptive content as the result of individualized analysis based on big data that is focused on the micro-performance of an individual rather than the overall data of an entire cohort. A.I. can drill down and analyze the knowledge base informed by big data and the cognitive ability according to an individual's learning behavior and uses the results to provide individualized learning content that accelerates development.

User Assessment

Research shows that knowledge assessment isn't optimized through intense, summative assessments and is better incorporated into ongoing, short, and targeted evaluation. However, before introducing A.I., many educators found it laborious to integrate formative assessment tasks and monitor each individual's results throughout their training programs. Now that A.I. can automate much of the process, implementing this type of assessment is gaining traction (Surve & Londhe, 2020). A.I.-based assessment quickly and accurately marks multiple-choice, fill in the blanks, and many other types of assessments and provides continuous feedback as learners progress.

Luckin (2017) discusses the use of A.I. for assessment and suggests that far more data can be collected and analyzed than the simple pass/fail of traditional assessments. She notes that a learner's emotional state and motivation can also be assessed by A.I., drawing a more well-rounded picture of the learner's current state and further training requirements. However, it is also noted that there are many types of assessment (some using A.I. and others not using A.I.) that should be included to gather varied data (Luckin, 2017). This helps to build a deeper understanding of the learner in the context of their broader environment.

Training Evaluation

A.I. can automate information collection and generate feedback which can streamline the training evaluation process. Data analytics can provide insights, identify effective courses and training elements, and pinpoint areas for improvement. In the workplace, A.I. can extract data to offer real-time insights that can enhance organizational productivity and decision-making (Ifenthaler, 2020) and lead to incremental improvements to training throughout the organization.

Analyzing the effectiveness of a training program is crucial but also very time-consuming; therefore, optimizing A.I. to collect and analyze data quickly can assist. Once accurate details are collected, they can then be considered through such lenses as the Kirkpatrick Evaluation Model (Reio Jr., Rocco, Smith, & Chang, 2017; Rodríguez-Pérez, 2013) to develop training initiatives that are effective and impactful and tie directly to measurable business outcomes.

In summary, considering the abovementioned elements that can be enhanced by A.I., it is undeniable that it will significantly improve current ways of working and learning. With improvements to the speed and accuracy of training needs analysis, content development, adaptive content, user assessment, and training evaluation, A.I. is improving learning opportunities across the workplace.

Scenario #3: The Agile Adaptors

Another prediction for the future workplace is defined by the World Economic Forum (2018) as organizations they refer to as 'Agile Adaptors.' In this scenario, workers will adapt to changes with agility, gaining core competencies that allow them to problem solve, collaborate, personalize their own working day, and construct their own professional development pathways. In this environment, the ethos for lifelong learning enhances enthusiasm and control over one's journey. As a result, productivity and creativity rise, leading to an agile workforce, that share ideas, technologies, products, services, and values.

The World Economic Forum (WEF) has identified a range of actions that organizations and individuals can take to proactively shape their future as agile adaptors (WEF, 2018) (Figure 4.4). These actions include:

1. The need for reskilling in the workplace.
2. Enhanced digital technologies, including mobile platforms.
3. Guidelines for collaborative, remote, and virtual work practices.

In addition to these, an agile learning design framework is imperative to support workplace learning. Seufert and Meier (2016) outline prominent frameworks for learning design in the agile workplace, which include the commonly used ADDIE (Analysis, Design, Development, Implementation, and Evaluation) model. Though they concede that the progressive approach of the Successive Approximation Model (SAM) (Figure 4.5) has become a more appropriate framework for the agile environment of the future workplace. (However, it is worth noting that the ADDIE model has its merits and can achieve quality outcomes, though its stage-by-stage process somewhat restricts it. In contrast, SAM has been developed to embrace a more agile methodology).

Similar to the previously mentioned HCD approach, the first stage of SAM is the preparation phase, which aims to rapidly gather information about learners' strengths and weaknesses and establish goals

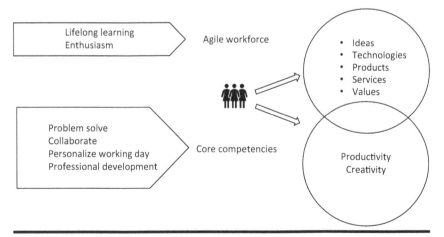

Figure 4.4   The agile adaptors. Adapted from the World Economic Forum (2018).

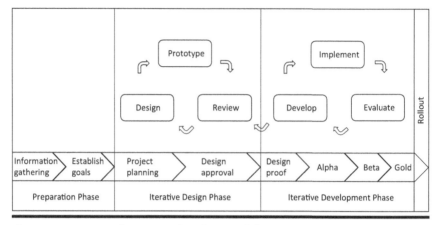

Figure 4.5 Successive Approximation Model (SAM). Adapted from Wintarti and Fardah (2019).

for the project. The conclusion of this phase requires key stakeholders to collaborate by brainstorming the training program's design (Seufert & Meier, 2016). The main takeaway here is that learners take ownership of the process and are more likely to commit to the end outcomes.

The second stage is the iterative design phase, in which learning designers work with subject matter experts to further develop the learning materials and gain approval for the design from the original group of collaborators. This moves on to the iterative development phase, where the team functions in a similar way to software developers working in sprint cycles, developing, implementing, and evaluating before moving onto the next iteration. The fourth and final stage is the alpha, beta, gold release. Alpha acts as a dry run that ensures the training course has been created as intended, and during which time changes can still be made through a feedback loop. Beta is like the pilot program, where a small group of users will run through the course from end to end before the gold release in which the training project is fully deployed (Jung, Kim, Lee, & Shin, 2019).

Other strategies were evaluated in a McKinsey and Company (2018) report on the five trademarks of agile organizations, in which they state that one of these trademarks is 'Rapid Decision and Learning Cycles.' In this rapid cycle, they suggest shifting the mindset from 'clear decisions and certainty,' to 'embrace uncertainty, own the process and be nimble and productive in trying new approaches.'

This continuous learning and development cycle encourages workers to innovate and carry out operations in an agile way. This model's characteristics focus on rapid sprints and experimentation; they develop standardized ways of working, such as communication channels, processes, and meeting formats, and promote transparency of information within and across teams. There is an emphasis on quick decision-making and an understanding of which stakeholders should be involved in making specific decisions. Continuous learning is a constant part of the agile company's DNA. This is demonstrated through peer and shadow learning, iterative formal learning, and adjustments made as new knowledge or experiences come to light.

Succession Approximation Model

Like any instructional system design, the SAM is a framework that systematically organizes instruction material and delivery. The differing aspect of SAM to other frameworks is the agile methodology that underpins it. Its goal is to take small, flexible steps within a larger framework to achieve outcomes. The rapid design and development approach uses shortened agile measures to bring solutions to the end user to gain feedback and improve the solution throughout, rather than at the end of its development lifecycle. The word 'approximation' depicts the iterative prototypes, as they serve as approximations of the final product, reducing the risk of developing costly solutions that have, in some way, missed the mark. The model allows for quick iterations to be delivered to stakeholders to be tested and challenged so they drive the final product's design.

There are several reasons that instructional designers are leaning toward the SAM in recent years, such as:

— It provides more realistic prototypes to base decisions on.
— There are multiple people involved, providing their unique perspectives.
— The small iterations during development allow for evaluation and changes to be made where necessary.
— Problems can be discovered before they have been unnecessarily embedded into the learning program.

However, it is important to remember that the SAM may not be ideal for everyone. There may be stakeholders, designers, and developers who are not comfortable with the lack of structure and prefer to have a definite outcome from the beginning. There are also teams who may not be willing to invest the time into collaboration and taking ownership of the ongoing development.

The three main stages of SAM, which work in a cyclical motion, are (1) the preparation phase, (2) the iterative design phase, and (3) the iterative development phase.

The Preparation Phase

Like the popular ADDIE model, which begins with the analysis phase, the preparation phase analyzes requirements and collects data to support the solution. The content and scope of this phase are likely to vary significantly depending on the needs of the project. However, it will always include gathering information about the learners' prior knowledge and the company's goals for the training.

At the end of the preparation phase is SAM's hallmark SAVVY Start. The SAVVY Start serves as an opportunity for all stakeholders to brainstorm, sketch and prototype the potential instructional designs. Prototypes are kept simple, using tools such as storyboards or drawings that can later serve as a backbone for further design sessions. After the SAVVY Start, stakeholders should have potential design ideas for each content area they wish to deliver.

The Iterative Design Phase

The iterative design phase aims to design and prototype the material to deliver something tangible to key stakeholders for evaluation. During this phase, the team will be reduced to involve subject matter experts, designers, and developers, who should aim to create three potential designs for each content area so that creativity extends beyond the more obvious design solutions. Roles should be clearly defined among the group to determine who is responsible for scripting, storyboarding, and instructional planning.

The iterative design phase always commences after the SAVVY Start so that expectations are in place. It is also helpful to have clearly set timelines, budgets, and roles and responsibilities defined at this point. Once the planning and additional design are complete, the team will refine the design and instructional collateral.

The Iterative Development Phase

As the team moves into the iterative development phase, the agreed-upon design progresses through a cycle of development, implementation, and evaluation. This phase focuses on developing small elements of the completed project to allow these components to be moved into the implementation/evaluation stages. This is where SAM and its agile groundings become more apparent, as there is always something usable being delivered to the end users to evaluate, and the feedback is fed back into the development loop as further iterations are made.

As the product moves through these iterations, three clear stages are known as the alpha, beta, and gold releases. The Alpha release is when all learning elements are usable from end to end, allowing stakeholders to interact with the course and check there are no significant issues. During this phase, feedback can still be provided, and editing can still occur. The beta stage occurs after this, where the product is in its final form, and it is released to a small pilot group of learners who can engage with the content and ensure everything is working as it is intended. Finally, the gold stage is where the final product is fully deployed.

Overall, if working in an agile workplace, the SAM provides the most agile instructional design practices that can complement these ways of working.

How Can Workplace Learning Adapt?

Due to the speed and nature of change within the workplace, it is imperative that learning and development teams not only adapt but keep ahead of the curve. Moving forward, those who are most likely to be successful in the future workplace are those who can adapt to agile ways of working and continuous change. Ongoing learning opportunities will become embedded in company strategy, and agile leaders will be highly valued as they demonstrate their ability to coach their workers through continuous development.

While the agile methodology has its origins in software development, it is being borrowed by various industries and functions, resulting in significant improvements in productivity and time to project completion (Cooper & Sommer, 2018). Agile has been found to be readily adaptable to learning and development operations due to the inclusive ownership of outcomes and the collaborative nature of the work (Krehbiel et al., 2017). Such milestones as planning, analysis, design, implementation, testing, and integration are incorporated in an ongoing cycle as incremental steps are made toward larger learning goals.

Learning is a process of discovery and can be subjective to the personal paradigm of the learner. As such, a learner is better placed when they can operate in various contexts and experiences and create meaningful knowledge. Instructors who value collaboration are transparent, inclusive, and provide ongoing feedback. Engagement, cooperation, and contribution from the group of learners lead to more extensive and contextual learning experiences. Krehbiel et al. (2017) suggest that this agile and collaborative approach produces better results than any individual can achieve alone.

By adopting an adaptive mindset, instructors can respond to uncertain and turbulent environments and modify their approach accordingly. As outlined by Briggs (2014), some of the characteristics of agile learning include:

— A high priority on satisfying the needs of the individual through the continuous evaluation of learning.
— Adaptive to changing requirements, updating learning approaches and harnessing changes accordingly.
— Frequent delivery of smaller, targeted learning modules.
— The creation of inclusive, self-directed learning experiences.
— Supportive environments where meaningful learning is a primary measure of progress.
— Learning that takes place at a constant and continuous pace.
— Teams that reflect incrementally on the progress made so they can adapt and adjust to improve their performance.

Future Directions for Workplace Learning

The digital revolution has transformed and continues to transform how we work, learn, and progress as individuals and as a broader society. Consideration is given not only to the fundamental changes of what people need to learn but how they learn it and how they apply it. Organizations, educators, and individuals are evolving their strategies and rethinking how learning paths are structured.

The three possibilities discussed above are scenarios that are already becoming our reality and continue to strengthen as technology progresses. The HCD approach empowers individuals to take control of their own learning journey, and the integrated A.I. scenario sees workers evolve to expand their skillsets and continually learn new ways of working. The agile adaptors focus on rapid learning cycles to keep up with evolving technologies.

The old paradigms of single-function roles, linear education, and one set of skills for life can no longer exist in these times of rapid digital advancement. Instead, organizations and individuals who embrace the paradigm shift to emphasize continuous improvement and lifelong learning will not only endure but will excel now and into the future.

Critical Thinking Questions

1   Why is organizational learning so important in the workplace of the future, regardless of the predicted scenario?
2   When designing new training programs, how does the HCD approach meet the requirements of learners in the workplace?
3   There are always two sides to the artificial intelligence argument. What is the likely future of A.I. in the workplace, and how can potential issues be mitigated?
4   Several positive aspects of workplace training are enabled by artificial intelligence, including adaptive content and improved assessment. Do the positive impacts outweigh the potential adverse effects of A.I. on the future workplace?
5   Why are agile practices increasing in popularity across the workforce, and is this methodology appropriate for designing and delivering workplace learning?

References

Belinski, R., Peixe, A. M. M., Frederico, G. F., & Garza-Reyes, J. A. (2020). Organizational learning and industry 4.0: Findings from a systematic literature review and research agenda. *Benchmarking: An International Journal.* Advance online publication. DOI:10.1108/BIJ-04-2020-0158
Briggs, S. (2014). *Agile-based learning: What is it, and how can it change education?* InformED. Retrieved from https://www.opencolleges.

edu.au/informed/features/agile-based-learning-what-is-it-and-how-can-it-change-education/

Cooper, R. G., & Sommer, A. F. (2018). Agile–stage–gate for manufacturers: Changing the way new products are developed integrating agile project management methods into a stage-gate system offers both opportunities and challenges. *Research-Technology Management*, *61*(2), 17–26. DOI:10.1080/08956308.2018.1421380

Flores, E., Xu, X., & Lu, Y. (2020). A reference human-centric architecture model: A skill-based approach for education of future workforce. *Procedia Manufacturing*, *48*, 1094–1101. DOI:10.1016/j.promfg.2020.05.150

Harari, Y. (2019). *21 lessons for the 21st century*. UK: Random House

Ifenthaler, D. (2020). Change management for learning analytics. In N. Pinkwart & S. Liu (Eds.), *Artificial intelligence supported educational technologies* (pp. 261–272). Cham, Switzerland: Springer.

Isotani, S., Millan, E., Ogan, A., Hastings, P., McLaren, B., & Luckin, R. (Eds.). (2019). *Artificial intelligence in education: 20th International Conference, AIED 2019, Chicago, IL, USA, June 25–29, 2019, Proceedings, Part I*. Springer. Retrieved from Retrieved from https://link.springer.com/book/10.1007%2F978-3-030-23204-7

Jung, H., Kim, Y., Lee, H., & Shin, Y. (2019). Advanced instructional design for successive E-learning: based on the successive approximation model (SAM). *International Journal on E-Learning*, *18*(2), 191–204.

Kelly, K. (2017). *The inevitable – Understanding the 12 technological forces that will shape our future*. USA: Penguin Group

Knapp, J. (2016). *Sprint. How to solve big problems and test new ideas in just five days*. New York: Random House.

Krehbiel, T. C., Salzarulo, P. A., Cosmah, M. L., Forren, J., Gannod, G., Havelka, D., … & Merhout, J. (2017). Agile manifesto for teaching and learning. *Journal of Effective Teaching*, *17*(2), 90–111.

Lin, J., Zhao, Y., Liu, C., & Pu, H. (2020). Personalized learning service based on big data for education. In *2020 IEEE 2nd International Conference on Computer Science and Educational Informatization (CSEI)* (pp. 235–238). Xinxiang, China: IEEE.

Luckin, R. (2017). Towards artificial intelligence-based assessment systems. *Nature Human Behaviour*, *1*(3), 1–3. DOI:10.1038/s41562-016-0028

Maguire, M. (2001). Methods to support human-centred design. *International Journal of Human-Computer Studies*, *55*(4), 587–634. DOI:10.1006/ijhc.2001.0503

McKinsey & Company. (2018). *Reimagining the post-pandemic organization*. McKinsey & Company. Retrieved from https://www.mckinsey.com/business-functions/organization/our-insights/reimagining-the-post-pandemic-organization#

Meier, J. J., & Miller, R. K. (2016). Turning the revolution into an evolution: The case for design thinking and rapid prototyping in libraries. *College & Research Libraries News*, *77*(6), 283–286. DOI:10.5860/crln.77.6.9506

Nguyen, J. (2020). *A human's guide to the future*. Pan Macmillan: Australia.

Price, Waterhouse, Coopers. (2018). *Workforce of the future: the yellow world in 2030*. Price Waterhouse Coopers. Retrieved December 10 2020 from https://www.pwc.com/gx/en/services/people-organisation/publications/workforce-of-the-future/workforce-of-the-future--the-yellow-world-in-2030.html

Reio, T. G., Jr., Rocco, T. S., Smith, D. H., & Chang, E. (2017). A critique of Kirkpatrick's evaluation model. *New Horizons in Adult Education & Human Resource Development, 29*(2), 35–53.

Rodríguez-Pérez José. (2013). The Kirkpatrick model for training effectiveness evaluation. In *CAPA for the FDA-regulated Industry*. Wisconsin, USA: American Society for Quality (ASQ).

Romero, D., Noran, O., Stahre, J., Bernus, P., & Fast-Berglund, Å. (2015). Towards a human-centred reference architecture for next-generation balanced automation systems: Human-automation symbiosis. In *IFIP International Conference on Advances in Production Management Systems* (pp. 556–566). Springer.

Seufert, S., & Meier, C. (2016). From eLearning to digital transformation: A framework and implications for L&D. *International Journal of Corporate Learning, 9*(2), 27–33. DOI:10.3991/ijac.v9i2.6003

Southgate, E. (2020). *Artificial intelligence, ethics, equity, and higher education*. National Centre for Student Equity in Higher Education: Curtin University. Retrieved from https://www.ncsehe.edu.au/artificial-intelligence-ethics-equity-higher-education/

Surve, B. C., & Londhe, B. R. (2020). Artificial intelligence based assessment and development of student's non-cognitive skills in professional education through an online learning management system. In *International Conference on Inventive Systems and Control (ICISC)* (pp. 329–336). IEEE. DOI:10.1109/ICISC47916.2020.9171137

Wintarti, A., & Fardah, D. K. (2019). The instructional design of blended learning on differential calculus using successive approximation model. *Journal of Physics: Conference Series, 1417*(1), 012064. IOP Publishing.

World Economic Forum. (2018). *Eight future of work: Scenarios and their implications*. World Economic Forum. Retrieved from http://www3.weforum.org/docs/WEF_FOW_Eight_Futures.pdf

Yuan, X. (2019). Model and implementation of personalized adaptive learning and analysis technology based on large data. In *2019 International Conference on Artificial Intelligence and Advanced Manufacturing (AIAM)* (pp. 202–205). Dublin, Ireland: IEEE.

Chapter 5

Technological Frameworks for Success

As technology in the workplace has made rapid advancements, so too have digitally enhanced learning opportunities. However, many companies have yet to implement or revise their ongoing learning programs and leverage such technologies. By starting with a technology-enabling framework, organizations are set up with the right infrastructure, resources, company policies, and programs for a successful future. As a result, learning and development professionals can feel confident that, despite ongoing changes, the foundation of provisions for quality learning will support evolving requirements.

Many technological models enable businesses to harness effective learning opportunities. Below, three specific frameworks have been selected for their relevance to the workplace of the future. The Learning Ecosystem Framework 2.0, the Technology-Enhanced Learning Framework, and the Digital Workplace Skills Framework provide solid foundations for technology-enabled workplace learning.

Framework #1 – The Learning Ecosystem Framework 2.0

The term 'learning ecosystem' has recently increased in popularity and includes the people, technologies, culture, content, and strategies that impact learning across an organization (Eudy, 2018). The ecosystem includes internal influences such as policies, culture, and business strategies and external influences such as formal qualifications, sources of public information, and workers from external companies (Redmond & Macfadyen, 2020).

According to Eudy (2018), due to the fast pace of digital change, current workplace skillsets have an average shelf life of around five years, making it imperative for employees to learn on an ongoing basis. Therefore, it is refreshing to examine the *Learning Ecosystem Framework 2.0* (which Redmond and Macfadyen developed) as there are many organizations that, to date, don't seem to realize this or actively prepare for a successful future as a learning organization.

Learning ecosystems do not leave learning to chance. Companies that adopt this type of framework consciously expose their workforce to ongoing and challenging experiences that enhance workers and their role. Redmond and Macfadyen's proposed framework support this while providing a flexible model that allows an organization to customize their ecosystem according to their requirements (Figure 5.1).

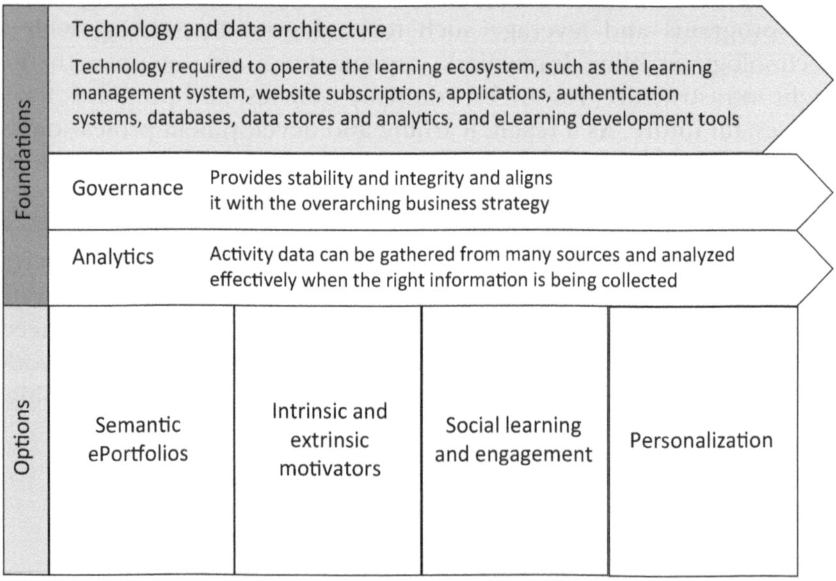

Figure 5.1 The Learning Ecosystem Framework 2.0, information. Adapted from Redmond and Macfadyen (2020).

The proposed Learning Ecosystem Framework 2.0 (LEF 2.0) is made up of seven key elements which are discusses as follows:

Technology and Data Architecture

The foundation of this learning ecosystem is the technology and data architecture, which must be at the forefront of design considerations. This design requires the most significant monetary investment as it will form the core of the learning framework that aligns with company strategy. Company and learner goals should drive the technology, rather than the technology driving the goals (dependent on what is possible).

The technology architecture includes all technology required to operate the learning ecosystem, such as the learning management system, website subscriptions, applications, authentication systems, databases, data stores and analytics, and eLearning development tools (Redmond & Macfadyen, 2020).

Particular attention should be paid to the design of the data architecture as this is where quality data can be gathered to provide significant business insights and inform improved ways of learning. The learning management system must be supplemented with external technologies to ensure currency, flexibility, and scalability (Redmond & Macfadyen, 2020), which should be guided by standards such as xAPI. By utilizing xAPI standards, the LMS can gather data on various touchpoints within the ecosystem (Eradze, Rodriguez-Triana, & Laanpere's, 2017; Foreman, 2013). Implementing a quality technology architecture and a quality data architecture will directly affect elements 3–7 of the LEF 2.0 and include data sources, stores, models, logistics, and processes (Redmond & Macfadyen, 2020).

Governance

A robust governance model for the learning ecosystem not only provides stability and integrity and aligns it with the overarching business strategy but provides significant credibility and 'buy-in' from executives. A governance body for the learning ecosystem is put in place to guide the direction, manage internal influences and react to external impacts (Redmond & Macfadyen, 2020). The governance team comprises key stakeholders whose role would be to oversee the company learning strategy, project planning, investment, architecture, policies, expenses, and evaluation (Alaeddini & Kardan, 2010).

Analytics

User activity data can be gathered from many sources and analyzed effectively when the right information is being collected. Considering what data should be captured is central to the ecosystem's overall design and hinges on sound data architecture. Redmond and Macfadyen (2020) outline some of the key metrics to include:

1. Data that reveals how the learning ecosystem is tracking alongside company goals, as this is useful for the governance team.
2. Academic analytics concerned with knowledge and skills from the individual to the broader ecosystem as this is useful to instructors, systems administrators, the governance team, and the individual learner.
3. Learning insights that measure, analyze, and report on learner data as these are useful for course instructors, designers, and developers.
4. Predictive analytics information to identify patterns and inform predictions of future behavior. These analytics greatly assist the end user and are also crucial for instructors, system administrators, and the governance team.

Semantic ePortfolios

While there is merit in the ideas around integrating learning analytics with ePortfolios to provide an ongoing profile of workplace-based assessment and feedback (Van der Schaaf et al., 2017), employers may err on the side of caution when investing resources into implementing such a profile that may not be carried over from one employer to another.

Within the proposed LEF 2.0, there are two ways in which information can be added to a semantic ePortfolio. The first being that workers can upload their own items for inclusion, such as presentations, videos, and documents and the second method is through thoughtful data extraction (Koraneekij & Khlaisang, 2015).

There is little evidence to suggest that in the workplace, this type of idea is willingly adopted and perpetuated by employees and is, therefore perhaps something that could be incorporated into more structured national and international standards in the future. There are existing ePortfolio environments that are utilized internationally, particularly in Europe (Van der Schaaf et al., 2017), though the uptake and consistency at this stage may still be underwhelming.

Intrinsic and Extrinsic Motivators

To assist in the motivation for workplace learning, Redmond and Macfadyen (2020) consider the influence of intrinsic (i.e., challenge, curiosity, and control) and extrinsic (i.e., competition and recognition) factors in their learning ecosystem. When an individual is intrinsically motivated, it is because they find the activity interesting and enjoyable and can see the personal growth and satisfaction they can obtain. In contrast, extrinsic motivation is impacted by external influences such as financial gain, status, or recognition. Therefore, consideration of the preferred motivational factors should be included in planning the learning ecosystem and then monitored and managed by the governance team.

Social Learning and Engagement

Another consideration during the design phase of the learning ecosystem is to include (and invest in where necessary) learning resources that promote collaboration. Humans are naturally social beings who can be motivated by one another to participate in activities and learning experiences in the workplace. If the company culture fosters social learning, individuals can encourage one another and share their learning experiences. Though it is worth noting that this is not always the case, and some people remain competitive and guarded when sharing (or withholding) their knowledge (Griffin & Burns, 2018).

Redmond and Macfadyen (2020) also discuss the relevance of social platforms such as the company Intranet and LinkedIn that allow for networking and sharing ideas. They also suggest integrating learning experience platforms such as Degreed, in which learners can be influenced by recommendations from others or by star-rated reviews that encourage (or discourage) them to engage with particular learning content. Knowledge sharing can result in workers gaining broader perspectives and becoming more informed on a variety of topics within the organization (Bingham & Conner, 2010).

Personalization

There are two aspects to personalization in this proposed learning ecosystem which are the personalization of the learning environment and personalized adaptive learning (Redmond & Macfadyen, 2020). The personalization of the learning environment is when an individual or the learning designer selects preferences such as content types, interface customizations, software and devices used to deliver learning programs. This leads to dynamic and robust environments that support collaborative, flexible, and personalized learning (Mershad & Wakim, 2018).

The second aspect, which is personalized adaptive learning, adjusts content, sequencing, and assessment to the individual's needs and keeps lessons relevant and engaging (Peng, Ma, & Spector, 2019).

Finally, Redmond and Macfadyen (2020) recommend implementing their proposed LEF 2.0 in stages with the initial focus on designing sound technology and data architecture, establishing governance, and defining and capturing relevant metrics. Once the organization has established these elements, it can proceed to incorporate the additional components most relevant to its objectives, considering semantic ePortfolios, intrinsic and extrinsic motivators, social learning and engagement, and personalization (Redmond & Macfadyen, 2020). This learning ecosystem considers internal influences such as policies, culture, and business strategies. Also outside influences such as workers' previous or externally acquired knowledge and external suppliers (Redmond & Macfadyen, 2020). At the same time it remains flexible and supports ongoing learning and development.

Framework #2 – The Technology-Enhanced Learning Framework

Technology-enhanced learning (TEL) is the purposeful integration of digital technologies in face-to-face and online learning environments. While TEL is used in various contexts, for the purpose of this analysis, we look at a general approach to leveraging digital technologies in the workplace to complement and improve learning outcomes. The aim is not only to understand the convenience and breadth of options offered by technological advancements but also to increase worker capabilities such as digital literacies, critical thinking, and collaboration. It also aims to improve the ability to integrate learning analytics which helps to inform targeted learning programs (Figure 5.2).

Many organizations are leveraging TEL in the workplace due to cost reduction, flexibility, and accessibility. However, Wang (2011) suggests that a common issue with the implementation of TEL programs is that they fail to align with overall company strategy, which

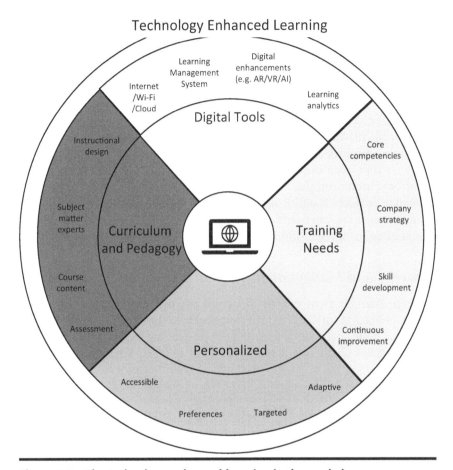

Figure 5.2   The technology-enhanced learning in the workplace.

can lead to a poorer perception of its potential. Therefore, given the importance of both digital skills and learning in the workplace, the alignment to overall organizational strategy is paramount to delivering successful TEL programs.

Volungeviciene, Teresevičienė, and Tait (2014) studied the integration of TEL in several organizational settings, which is discussed below. They identified seven essential principles identified as follows (Volungeviciene et al., 2014):

1. Strategy and management
2. Information communication technologies and infrastructure

3. Continuous professional development
4. Technology-enhanced learning curriculum
5. Support systems
6. Quality assurance
7. Marketing and business development.

While it is clear that the implementation of TEL needs careful and systematic planning to ensure success, it is first worth noting that Volungeviciene et al. (2014) point out that there is limited research to draw on that examines the implementation of TEL into business organizations, including the associated issues, constraints, and challenges. However, studies have observed that organizational learning culture, management support, and organizational policy play crucial roles in the successful integration of TEL (Figure 5.3).

Strategy and Management

Change management serves a significant purpose in the successful implementation of TEL in the workplace, assisting smooth transitions to new ways of working and improving workers' perception of usefulness and ease of use (Davis, 1989; Kim, Park, & Lee, 2007).

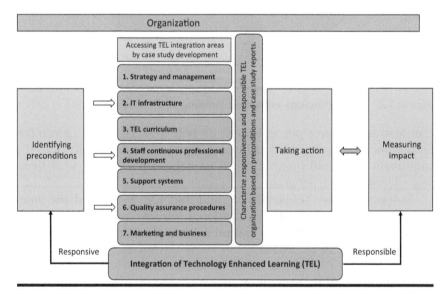

Figure 5.3   Framework of TEL integration into an organization. Adapted from Volungeviciene et al. (2014).

The psychological factors for technology acceptance include, but are in no way limited to, the cognitive response of the user, the affective response (attitude toward using the technology), and the behavioral response (the actual use of the system) (Davis & Sumara, 2001). Change management practices are fully engaged in the entire planning and implementation of successful TEL integrations. Strategies for such integration can include end-user involvement in pre-initiation and initiation, providing bottom-up experiences during the implementation, and enabling a workplace culture of acceptance.

It has been noted by Hamburg and Hall (2008) in their studies that many businesses, particularly the small to medium enterprises, fail to implement effective TEL for the following reasons.

— They take a reactive approach to learning.
— They are unable to quickly locate quality electronic content.
— Generally, they have a lack of time to source relevant training options.
— The appropriate ICT applications are not in place.
— There is often an absence of staff motivation to participate.
— There is a general lack of understanding of the benefits of eLearning.

These challenges can be mitigated through effective change management practices that inform workers of the company's vision and the impacts of the TEL plans on the individual.

Information and Communication Technologies and Infrastructure

Volungeviciene et al. (2014) outline three types of technology necessary to implement TEL in the workplace. These are technology infrastructure including network facilities, database resources and connectivity, instructional technology to support facilitators, and instructional technology to support learners. In light of recent changes to workplaces (as a result of the COVID-19 pandemic), technology infrastructure is being considered differently than it was before. It can no longer be taken for granted that the technology infrastructure will be located at one single point, exclusively using onsite hardware.

Instructional technology to support facilitators includes learning management systems and associated tools, learning design software, and access to robust learning analytics. At the same time, instructional technology to support learners should be presented in the same package and include flexible features from sophisticated learning management systems or learning experience platforms.

Technology-Enhanced Learning Curriculum

A technology-enhanced curriculum should be synchronized with an organization's values, strategies, and operations while providing learning opportunities that enhance real-life working experiences. It is difficult to deny that the 21st century workplace is entrenched and reliant on digital technologies, and therefore, internal learning curriculums should reflect the same.

The successful implementation of a TEL curriculum requires a digitally positive mindset and a commitment to continuously learning how to advance as new capabilities become available. Technology-enhanced curriculum design has shifted to become more user-centric, and education has become more autonomous, comprehensive, integrated, and ongoing, meaning that those who are capable and comfortable using technology will be more likely to access, understand, and apply what has been learned.

When developing activities enhanced by technology, it is important to consider open educational resources, activity scenarios, support, participants, epistemological consistency, self-assessment, acceptable IT tools, didactic consistency, copyright, reusability, and accessibility. All of which play an important role in the quality of TEL curriculums (Volungeviciene et al., 2014).

Continuing Professional Development

Ultimately, the success of TEL will come down to the willingness and ability of workers to utilize them to develop their professional skills and knowledge. This should be implemented and encouraged by adjusting methods suitable to both the individual and the company's needs. Strategic company planning for the consistent development of its workforce will improve overall company results. However, the individual takes accountability for their own outcomes, despite the technologies and the curriculum that are offered.

TEL aims to be engaging, flexible, and learner-focused, enabling workers to leverage mobile devices and other tools to assist in learning at a time and place that suits them best. This practice allows the learner to take a self-directed approach that is more likely to suit their needs and keep them motivated.

Support Systems

The most effective way to mitigate adverse impacts on successful TEL is to provide a quality support system. Learners who have access to an instructor and their peers and guidance materials are more supported throughout the learning experience. However, Volungeviciene et al. (2014) stress the importance of properly planning and organizing such support.

Support types to consider should include administrative, pedagogical, and technical support (Graham, Woodfield, & Harrison, 2013). With these three types of support in place, the learner can overcome roadblocks regarding how to access resources, how to engage with and understand the course content, and how to optimize the use of technology.

Quality Assurance Procedures

As with all good business practices, quality assurance procedures should be embedded across the operations of all parts of the organization, including the effective use of TEL. Proper quality assurance measures include tools and resources that are attributed to individual implementation steps and clearly identify the factors that could affect the implementation strategy.

There is limited research available to suggest benchmarks that support the update of quality assurance procedures for TEL. However, the inclusion of quality assurance procedures gives parameters and credibility to the planning of TEL and also improves the perception and adoption of the technology.

Marketing and Business

While learning and development teams may clearly understand and value TEL, this is not necessarily the case for the remainder of the business. Many people have little information about why they should engage in ongoing learning opportunities and the role that digital technology can play to make learning easier.

Internal marketing is an often overlooked but valuable step in the deployment of TEL across the workplace. By sending out frequent and engaging communications, providing demonstrations, use cases, Q&As, and reminders, this can attract workers to the benefits of TEL and help them to understand how and why to access these learning opportunities.

Overall, TEL in the workplace harnesses the workforce's ongoing development and continuously aims to improve upon the best available technological practices. It involves the strategic integration of digital technologies that will serve the workplace to improve learning outcomes. By setting up an effective TEL system, learning and development professionals can deliver and monitor significant learning opportunities to enhance capabilities across the organization.

Framework #3 – The Digital Workplace Skills Framework

Digital literacy, as first popularized by Gilster (1997), described the ability to understand and use information in multiple formats from a wide variety of sources when it is presented via computers and, particularly, through the medium of the Internet. The digital literacy framework is a well-known, tried, and tested framework that has evolved over time, and in this section, we analyze Marsh's (2018) variation she calls the Digital Workplace Skills Framework. In the organizations of today, advanced digital skills are becoming increasingly valued, and in the not-too-distant future, it will be absolutely vital to not only display basic digital skills but also demonstrate a mature skillset and high level of confidence with a wide variety of digital technologies.

Traditionally, 'literacy' described one's ability to read and write (which later expanded to include talking and listening) and has further progressed to include the ability to effectively evaluate information sources, interpret text, create interesting ways of presenting information, and communicate appropriately in a variety of situations. In the same way, the meaning of digital literacy has advanced from the mere ability to operate a computer and use basic word processing and internet skills to include the ability to select appropriate applications for different requirements, collaborate using a variety of technologies, and ensure cyber safety. We are moving to a new landscape where digital 'citizens' are increasingly expected to collaborate, optimize, evaluate, and reflect on their digital practices while educating themselves on recent advancements and technologies as they emerge.

Due to the COVID-19 pandemic, as millions of workers shifted to working remotely (albeit temporarily), it brought to light the impact that a lack of digital skills can have on an organization. This was after alarming facts had already been realized, such as those reported by the House of Commons in the UK in 2016. This report claims that almost 50 percent of UK employers claim they have digital skill gaps in their businesses, costing an estimated 63 billion pounds a year to the UK economy (Marsh, 2018). Because this report was compiled before the pandemic, we can only guess how much wider that gap has grown due to rapid and unplanned decentralization. Companies that were digitally dexterous pre-2020 – what Soule, Puram, Westerman, and Bonnet (2016) describe as having the ability to move swiftly and as a whole to exploit new digital opportunities – were likely much better off when the crisis hit. Therefore, as digital literacy underpins the very nature of being able to learn online or within a blended learning program, it seems timely and fitting to include a good digital literacy framework as one to be considered for success.

The Digital Workplace Skills Framework developed by Marsh (2018) dissects the core skill areas and subfacets that make up a solid digital literacy framework to support workplace learning. Marsh (2018) explains this is a layered model that allows learners to transition through three stages. These stages are digital competence, digital usage, and digital transformation (Figures 5.4, 5.5).

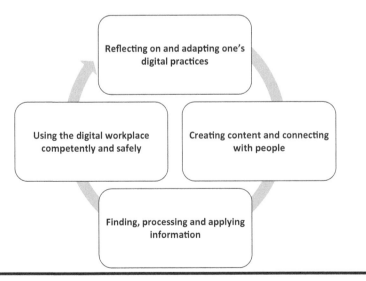

Figure 5.4   The digital workplace skills framework – overview. Adapted from Marsh (2018).

Using the digital workplace	Establish	The basic skills to use digital workplace devices and applications.
	Safeguard	Awareness of potential risks posed to both individuals and the organization.
	Optimize	Optimizing digital working environment in order to maximize productivity.
	Innovate	Leverage digital tools to create innovative ideas, solutions and ways of working.
Process & apply	Access	Navigate across disparate sources, and gain access to appropriate resources.
	Evaluate	Critically evaluate and interpret resources.
	Assimilate	Process a large amount of data from a range of sources.
	Apply	Leverage information to perform day-to-day tasks.
Create & connect	Create	Create new resources in a range of formats.
	Communicate	Communicate in the digital workplace using the most appropriate tools.
	Relate	Establish an appropriate digital identity.
	Collaborate	Work productively with others as part of a virtual team or community.
Think & adapt	Attend	Manage cognitive load in context of multiple real-time inputs and large quantities of information.
	Flex	Work flexibly, independently and effectively by adopting digital tools.
	Learn	Leverage learning opportunities in a digital workplace.
	Reflect	Reflect and improve on digital practices.

Figure 5.5 The digital workplace skills framework – elements. Adapted from Marsh (2018).

Marsh (2018) also describes four skill areas (each with four sub-facets) that make up the Digital Workplace Skills Framework:

Using Technology in the Workplace

There are four basic areas Marsh (2018) identifies in which employees can form the foundations of their digital literacy. These are (in order of increasing complexity): establish, safeguard, optimize, and innovate.

Establish

When a learner establishes their use of technology in the workplace, they build awareness of the tools and applications that are available and how they can be used to improve performance. For example, familiarity with desktop computer functionality, transferring information to the cloud to be accessed on mobile devices, and working with the company finance system may help a worker perform their tasks in the workplace in a basic way.

Safeguard

Workers who can safeguard their use of technology understand the risks involved with using computers and their associated applications, such as personal privacy and cyberattacks, and how they can mitigate these risks for the company and for themselves. For example, an employee understands the implications of a cyberattack, the risks of activities such as clicking links in externally received emails, maintaining respect for others online, and keeping their personal details secure.

Optimize

Workers optimize technology when they can appropriately select and configure the available digital tools to enhance their own working experience – for example, selecting various software applications, useful websites, and connecting Bluetooth devices such as headsets to increase efficiency.

Innovate

Building on foundational skills, individuals can configure and collaborate to produce new ways of using technology to enhance performance for themselves, their teams, and their organization. For example, working as a team to create an interactive presentation with accompanying staff survey to share on the company intranet before gathering and analyzing the data.

Processing and Applying Information

The amount of time spent searching for, curating, and evaluating information is substantial, with research suggesting that up to 20 percent of productivity can be lost (Roach, 1998) when data is not readily available. Marsh (2018) recognizes the need for workers to understand how to effectively find, process, and apply information and breaks down the necessary skillsets into four progressive areas.

Access

Skills in this area begin with the ability to clearly understand what information is being sought, identifying key search terms, and understanding where to search for information. This could include web browsers, databases, intranet files, and tools like email and chat history. Understanding where to search for particular information is often the first step in achieving search goals, and can lead to further opportunities for increased knowledge.

Evaluate

Digital evaluation skills include the ability to filter through information to determine what is best suited to the search. Some things to consider are (1) the validity of resources, that is, is the information part of a paid promotion? (2) The view of the author, is it influenced, credible, or bias? (3) The relevance of the information, is it in context, and can it relate to the instance at hand? And (4) the timeliness of the source, for example, was the information written in 1980 or 2020, and does this affect the accuracy of the information?

Assimilate

Once data is successfully accessed and evaluated, it then needs to be assimilated to fit the workplace practice. This includes downloading, storing, categorizing, and utilizing material in the appropriate context and understanding where and when to access and use certain information. These tools and materials are likely to enhance the work being produced as well as increasing the relevance of the outputs.

Apply

By applying knowledge, one can judge a situation and leverage the acquired resources to extract the most appropriate information for the task. It involves interpreting the available information in the most appropriate way for the context of the task at hand and understanding how to transfer that knowledge into workplace practice.

Create and Connect

Regardless of the industry, creating content in a variety of formats and collaborating with teams is essential. Communication is carried out through various online formats, and users understand how to form a positive online identity while also selecting the most appropriate platforms to carry their message. This includes the skills: create, communicate, relate, and collaborate.

Create

The creation of new content is essential for suitable communication on a variety of levels. Workers can create new resources in various formats and effectively use their digital literacy skills to interpret other people's creations. Workers can develop more meaningful and engaging communications and other artifacts through the use of digital technologies.

Communicate

Communication skills using digital technology are essential in the workplace and workers should be able to select the most relevant channels, methods, and guidelines. Digital communications work best when a company establishes clear exchange protocols throughout the organization (St. Amant, 2005).

Relate

Social tools can enable workers to build an online identity and network with others in appropriate ways. This reaches beyond the organization to include business partners and clients and allows instant communication among team members and other groups. Digital literacy skills are imperative to safely and effectively leverage social media platforms to positively relate to others using the most suitable methods.

Collaborate

Effective connection in the workplace leads to positive collaboration. Working together and contributing to virtual teams, establishing trust, and sharing the ownership of creations are all higher-level digital literacy skills that can improve business outcomes. There are many technological solutions that allow multiple people to contribute to one piece of work, tracking changes and providing feedback, often in real time.

Think and Adapt

Marsh (2018) stresses the importance of evaluating and adjusting to new technologies and practices to allow for an optimal flow of information. Self-aware employees can personalize how they interact with digital environments enabling them to structure their own personalized experience. With the following skillsets, workers can truly enhance their working and learning practices by incorporating the use of technology.

Attend

To be attentive to what one is doing in the digital workplace means managing one's cognitive load when experiencing multiple inputs of data from different sources. Due to the vast and increasing number of inputs, including emails, notifications, and reminders, workers find themselves switching between tasks and require a higher-level of ability to stay focused and manage their workload. Therefore, managing attention by defining and focusing on the task at hand will streamline productivity and reduce complications that may result in errors or reworking.

Flex

Employees can work flexibly and independently by adopting appropriate digital tools to support their productivity. This skillset enables workers to understand their options and how to best select and utilize applications for their required outcomes. This can lead to increased productivity, enhanced ownership and even improved wellbeing in the workplace (Marsh, 2018). Flexibility is also more likely to come naturally when an employee is familiar with their workplace technologies and the applications they utilize, and particularly when they are experimental and interested in learning about new features or functionality that they may not have previously used.

Learn

Digital savvy workers can recognize and leverage ongoing learning opportunities through formal and informal avenues. By fostering this attitude, more workers are setting time and space to commit to continuous learning in the workplace. Learning and development professionals can assist by creating personalized development plans (Marsh, 2018) that will help workers to track their progress over time.

Reflect

By evaluating and reflecting on best practices, employees become aware of how to continue their development in the digital space. Being mindful of the available technology, the scope of what these technologies can do, and how they can improve their working life, workers can continue to adjust the technology landscape for their own personal work.

In summary, the Digital Workplace Skills Framework suggests assessing 16 digital skill areas and developing interventions to close the skill gaps. These should be done with clear alignment to company goals and work as a starting point for understanding what the organization will achieve by having a digitally literate workforce (Marsh, 2018). Further development and ongoing assessment of capabilities will help to properly evaluate the effects of digital literacy on the overall achievement of the organization and its workers. This is a technological framework that should successfully support digital literacy in the workplace if implemented and maintained effectively.

Conclusion

Due to the rapid advancements of technology in the workplace, the opportunities for digitally enhanced learning are twofold:

1. Learning how to use technology
2. Learning by using technology.

As an increasing number of organizations implement sophisticated learning programs, technological frameworks are more relevant than ever before.

Investing the time and money into the proper infrastructure, resources, policies, and programs, organizations can set themselves up for successful learning and development now and into the future. While many frameworks are suitable, above, we examined three potential technological frameworks that can work well for most modern enterprises. The Learning Ecosystem Framework 2.0, the Technology-Enhanced Learning Framework, and the Digital Workplace Skills Framework can provide foundations for learning while remaining flexible enough to be tweaked for the workplace's requirements. Implementing such frameworks is more relevant than ever since rapid changes have impacted how companies operate. These changes call for learning to come to the forefront of company strategy, and as we move into the future, learning programs that are firmly supported by technology are imperative.

Critical Thinking Questions

1   Redmond and Macfadyen (2020) recommend implementing the Learning Ecosystem Framework 2.0 in stages. Why is this advised?
2   In what ways can a governance body manage the internal and external influences on the Learning Ecosystem Framework 2.0?
3   How can a technology-enhanced curriculum be synchronized with an organization's values, strategies, and operations?
4   Why is digital literacy so important in the workplace? What comparisons can be drawn between the traditional need for literacy and the current requirement for digital literacy?
5   We understand that the technological landscape in the workplace is likely to remain fluid. In what ways does laying a solid foundation assist in adapting to new technologies as they advance?

References

Alaeddini, M., & Kardan, A. (2010). E-learning governance - Towards an applicable framework. In *2010 2nd International Conference on Education Technology and Computer* (Vol. *3*, pp. V3-529). IEEE. DOI:10.1109/ICETC.2010.5529486

Bingham, T., & Conner, M. (2010). *The new social learning: A guide to transforming organizations through social media*. California: Association for Talent Development.

Davis, F. D. (1989). Usefulness, perceived ease of use, and user acceptance of information technology. *MIS Quarterly*, *13*(3), 319–340. DOI:10.2307/249008

Davis, B., & Sumara, D. (2001). Learning communities: Understanding the workplace as a complex system. *New Directions for Adult and Continuing Education*, *2001*(92), 85–96. DOI:10.1002/ACE.43

Eradze, M., Rodriguez-Triana, M. J., & Laanpere, M. (2017). How to aggregate lesson observation data into learning analytics datasets? In L. P. Prieto, R. Martinez-Maldonado, D. Spikol, D. Hernández-Leo, Rodriguez-Triana, M. J., & X. Ochoa (Eds.), *Joint proceedings of the 6th multimodal learning analytics (MMLA) workshop and the 2nd cross-LAK workshop co-located with 7th international learning analytics and knowledge conference (LAK 2017)* (Vol. *1828*, pp. 74–81). Columbia, Canada: CEUR.

Eudy, R. (2018). What is a learning ecosystem? And how does it support corporate strategy? *Ej4*. Retrieved from https://www.ej4.com/blog/what-is-a-learning-ecosystem

Foreman, S. (2013). *The xAPI and the LMS: What does the future hold?* Learning Solutions. Retrieved from https://learningsolutionsmag.com/articles/1271/the-xapi-and-the-lms-what-does-the-future-hold

Gilster, P. (1997). *Digital literacy*. London: Wiley.

Graham, C. R., Woodfield, W., & Harrison, J. B. (2013). A framework for institutional adoption and implementation of blended learning in higher education. *The Internet and Higher Education, 18*, 4–14. DOI:10.1016/j.iheduc.2012.09.003

Griffin, M., & Burns, A. (2018). *The learning imperative: Raising performance in organisations by improving learning*. Wales, UK: Crown House Publishing.

Hamburg, I., & Hall, T. (2008). Informal learning and the use of Web 2.0 within SME training strategies. *eLearning Papers, 11*(2008). 28264232_Informal_learning_and_the_use_of_Web_2.0_within_SME_training_strategies

Kim, B. G., Park, S. C., & Lee, K. J. (2007). A structural equation modelling of the Internet acceptance in Korea. *Electronic Commerce Research and Applications, 6*(4), 425–432. DOI:10.1016/j.elerap.2006.08.005

Koraneekij, P., & Khlaisang, J. (2015). Development of learning outcome based eportfolio model emphasizing on cognitive skills in pedagogical blended e-learning environment for undergraduate students at faculty of education, Chulalongkorn University. *Procedia-Social and Behavioral Sciences, 174*, 805–813. Retrieved from https://doi.org/10.1016/j.sbspro.2015.01.664

Marsh, E. (2018). *The digital workplace skills framework: Ensuring the workforce is ready to work digitally*. Digital Work Research. Retrieved from https://digitalworkresearch.com/wp-content/uploads/2018/02/The-Digital-Workplace-Skills-Framework-final.pdf

Mershad, K., & Wakim, P. (2018). A learning management system enhanced with internet of things applications. *Journal of Education and Learning, 7*(3), 23–40. DOI:10.5539/jel.v7n3p23

Peng, H., Ma, S., & Spector, J.M. (2019). Personalized adaptive learning: An emerging pedagogical approach enabled by a smart learning environment. In M. Chang, E. Popescu, Kinshuk, N.-S. Chen, M. Jemni, R. Huang, J. M. Spector, & D. G. Sampson (Eds.), *Foundations and trends in smart learning. Lecture notes in educational technology* (pp. 171–176). Springer. DOI:10.1007/978-981-13-6908-7_24

Redmond, W., & Macfadyen, L. (2020). A framework to leverage and mature learning ecosystems. *International Journal of Emerging Technologies in Learning, 15*(5), 75–99. DOI:10.3991/ijet.v15i05.11898

Roach, S. (1998). In search of productivity. *Harvard Business Review, 76*(5), 153–160.

Soule, D. L., Puram, A. D., Westerman, G. F., & Bonnet, D. (2016). *Becoming a digital organization: The journey to digital dexterity*. SSRN. Retrieved from https://ssrn.com/abstract=2697688

St. Amant, K. (2005). Virtual office communication protocols: A system for managing international virtual teams. In *IPCC 2005. Proceedings. International Professional Communication Conference, 2005* (pp. 703–717). IEE. DOI:10.1109/IPCC.2005.1494242

Van der Schaaf, M., Donkers, J., Slof, B., Moonen-Van Loon, J., van Tartwijk, J., Driessen, E., … & Ten Cate, O. (2017). Improving workplace-based assessment and feedback by an E-portfolio enhanced with learning analytics. *Educational Technology Research and Development, 65*(2), 359–380. DOI:10.1007/s11423-016-9496-8

Volungeviciene, A., Teresevičienė, M., & Tait, A. W. (2014). Framework of quality assurance of TEL integration into an educational organization. *International Review of Research in Open and Distributed Learning, 15*(6), 211–236. DOI: 10.19173/irrodl.v15i6.1927

Wang, T. H. (2011). Developing web-based assessment strategies for facilitating junior high school students to perform self-regulated learning in an e-learning environment. *Computers & Education, 57*(2), 1801–1812. DOI:10.1016/j.compedu.2011.01.003

Chapter 6

Learning Analytics: Paving the Way to Improved Educational Outcomes

Learning analytics (LA) is an evidence-based approach to gathering and evaluating relevant data with the intention of improving learning outcomes. Data can originate from different sources, be stored in various formats, have varying levels of structure, and are usually used to enable decision-making (Samuelsen, Chen, & Wasson, 2019).

While there are varying descriptions depending on the context and purpose of LA, most literature tends to use the definition offered at the 1st International Conference on Learning Analytics (Association for Computing Machinery, 2011) and adopted by the Society for Learning Analytics Research (SoLAR) which is *"the measurement, collection, analysis, and reporting of data about learners and their contexts, for the purposes of understanding and optimizing learning and the environments in which it occurs."*

While the field of LA is emergent, it is gradually moving toward a state of maturity that positions it as a fundamental tool to support digital workplace learning. It sits at the convergence of education, analytics, and human-centered design (SoLAR, n.d.). LA aims to improve learner success by identifying the essential characteristics of the learning process, how to measure these characteristics, and how to use the measurements to inform best practice (Peña-Ayala, Cárdenas-Robledo, & Sossa, 2017).

This chapter will discuss the progress and potential of LA in the workplace and the trends that continue to influence its advancements, such as Experience API and adaptive learning. It will also examine the implications of its integration into the workplace, such as the barriers to adoption and the privacy and ethics associated with data collection.

Foundations of Learning Analytics

The standards for measurement in learning have historically focused on post-learning evaluation, whereas improved results can be obtained by utilizing data at all stages of the learning and development cycle. By examining the basic LA cycle, and the commonly used 'types' of LA, it becomes easier to follow specific methods to achieve particular goals.

There are variations to the LA model depending on the outcomes sought. Yuan (2019) suggests a basic preliminary model of LA as a circular process of data collection, analysis, feedback, intervention, and learning, while García-Peñalvo (2020) claims the foundational steps are data collection, data pre-processing, analytics, post-processing, and decision-making. Both of these models provide sound foundations for implementing LA into the workplace (Figures 6.1, 6.2).

The next thing to consider is the type of analytics required, such as descriptive, diagnostic, predictive, or prescriptive analytics. These methods use various facets to answer different kinds of questions with varying degrees of difficulty. Nitu, Dascalu, Lazarou, Trifan, and Bodea (2018) outline the following techniques in the order of increasing complexity (Figures 6.3):

1. Descriptive analytics – this is basic event data that displays what has happened, for example, the number of attendees, the percentage of a course they have completed, and their assessment scores.
2. Diagnostic analytics – is the next step of analysis that inquiries about why something happened, not just what happened.

For example, if there were low completion rates among a particular demographic, say, senior managers, in comparison to the completion rates of new starters, it may be that the course content is too basic for them, and an advanced course should be designed.

3. Predictive analytics – these explain what may be likely to happen. For example, a learner survey revealing eLearning users prefer not to access content on their desktop but rather their mobile device, which would inform the design of future modules that are more mobile-friendly.

4. Prescriptive analytics – is where solutions can be found about why something happened and what should be done as a result. For example, data may reveal that learners scored well in a theoretical assessment but lacked the ability to transfer the new skills to their work activities. Consequently, subsequent training may be provided as a practical on-the-job activity.

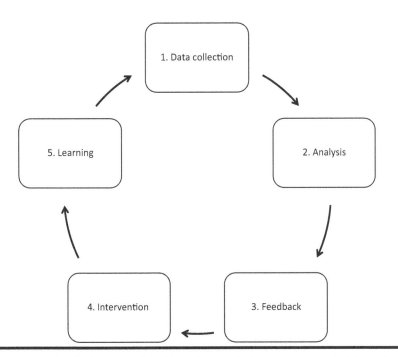

Figure 6.1   Preliminary model of learning analysis system. Adapted from Yuan (2019).

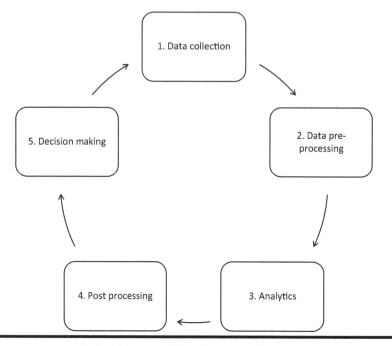

Figure 6.2 Foundational steps of learning analytics. Adapted from García-Peñalvo (2020).

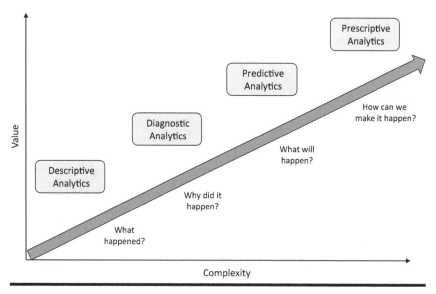

Figure 6.3 Types of data analytics, progressing in complexity.

Progress of Learning Analytics in the Workplace

In recent times, there has been much progress in the field of LA. Initially, LA was used to evaluate learning in the areas of school and higher education but has since expanded into the workplace, where it continues to evolve. As metrics become clearer and the use for LA in the workplace is more widely realized, businesses can see the value of its implementation. In addition to this, because data analytics in general areas such as sales and finance are captivating business audiences, it is becoming easier to transition such benefit realization to workplace learning.

Another progression for LA in the workplace is the introduction of external metrics, which allows data to be captured outside the primary learning management system. Data can originate from various sources, have different levels of structure, be stored in a variety of formats (Samuelsen et al., 2019), and be analyzed to reveal trends, correlations, and variations while highlighting problems and successes. Employee training designed with clear metrics in place, outlining the data to be collected regardless of the modality of the training, can be very effective for continuous improvement. By tracking data from a worker's engagement with digital technology and pairing this with skill goals, personalized learning can be delivered to assist individuals on their professional journeys (Dawson, Mirriahi, & Gasevic, 2015).

Eradze, Rodriguez Triana, and Laanpere (2017) carried out studies on how observational records can be integrated with activity-tracking data, which results in a multimodal dataset. The study identified the need for theoretical and pedagogical semantics when working with multimodal LA. In the same way, other data sources that are not embedded in a learning management system can be gathered for analysis, such as external training attendance, group participation, and the real-life application of skills.

The integration of multiple sources of data is reliant on four aspects; technical (services for data exchange), semantic (ensuring meaning is preserved and understood), legal (legal frameworks and policies), and organizational (company goals and requirements), and each of these contributes to the effectiveness of workplace LA (Samuelsen et al., 2019).

Current Potential for Learning Analytics in the Workplace

There is significant potential for LA in the workplace as it expands and brings about more significant learning and business opportunities. Along with business insights and employee benefits, LA can also identify why some training programs fail and how to use data and appropriate frameworks to revive them effectively. LA draws on a set of data and methodologies that can offer real-time, summative, and predictive insights to enhance learning, organizational productivity, and decision-making (Ifenthaler, 2020). It can be leveraged to create appropriate cognitive and administrative support for learners, leading to improved business outcomes.

LA in the workplace is also an action-oriented approach used to benefit employees. When learning programs are informed by quality LA and are measured and evaluated effectively, they can increase retention rates, productivity, skill levels, and loyalty. According to Bersin (2013), organizations that provide their employees with relevant, ongoing learning experiences have the edge over their competitors.

However, while the utilization of LA has been around for some time, it is reasonable to presume that there are still many companies that are generally constricting themselves by collecting data but not doing much in the way of analysis. The follow-up analysis is vital as the collection and assessment of data need to evolve beyond simply reporting on what has happened to making predictions about what could happen and subsequently offering appropriate recommendations.

There are several frameworks that incorporate the characteristics, methods, components, benefits, and issues that comprise LA. One such example is the Greller and Drachsler Framework for Learning Analytics (Greller & Drachsler, 2012) which categorizes six dimensions of LA, each of which they claim to be critical:

1. Stakeholder – This includes the beneficiaries of the LA process (such as the organization, the instructors, and the learners), the suppliers of data, and other agencies such as service providers and researchers. All stakeholders should be aware of the privacy and ethical considerations and other LA policies developed by the company.
2. Objective – In this context, two fundamental goals support the individual learning process. The first is reflection, which is the

critical self-evaluation enabled when individuals have access to their own datasets. The second is prediction, which is allowed when data is evaluated and consequently leads to adaptation and intervention.

3. Educational data – One of the main challenges with LA is the availability of quality datasets, including open and protected data sources. While open access to public data is highly controversial, some movements, such as the Open Access Publishing Movement, call for the wider availability of data (Drachsler et al., 2010). In the absence of open data, companies can rely on their own historical datasets, of which they have gained permission to use.

4. Instruments – Information retrieval technologies like data mining and statistical analysis can support LA objectives. In contrast, conceptual instruments like algorithms, theoretical constructs, and weightings can translate data into meaningful information.

5. External constraints – There are many external constraints related to conventions and norms regarding the implementation of LA in the workplace, including legal, logistical, and social regulations. There are also the growing implications of privacy and ethics that command monitoring and compliance.

6. Internal limitations – There is a high level of competence required for stakeholders tasked with interpreting data. Therefore, if not done correctly, it can lead to internal limitations, mainly because data can be interpreted in several different ways (Reffay & Chanier, 2003), and the acceptance of practice and results can also vary.

These six dimensions may be incorporated to varying degrees, but Greller and Drachsler (2012) stress the importance of considering each one individually within an LA plan (Figures 6.4).

Experience API

Experience API (xAPI) is an online software specification developed to allow a variety of learning systems to integrate in a manner that records a central repository of data in a Learning Record Store (Secretan, Wild, & Guest, 2019). For the purposes of LA in the workplace, xAPI can gather many metrics from different sources that allow more well-rounded and accurate tracking of learning outcomes throughout an organization (Figures 6.5).

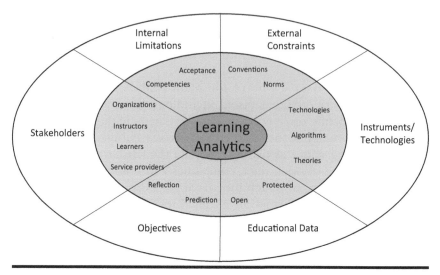

Figure 6.4   Greller and Drachsler framework for learning analytics. Adapted from Greller and Drachsler (2012).

Because quality data can come from many sources and is mined for various goals, the challenge lies with bringing these disparate sources together into a learning data repository (Williamson, 2014). The solution to this has come in the form of standards such as the Predictive Analytics Reporting (PAR) Framework, the Experience (x) API, the IMS Global Caliper Framework, and the Pittsburgh Science of Learning Center Data Shop.

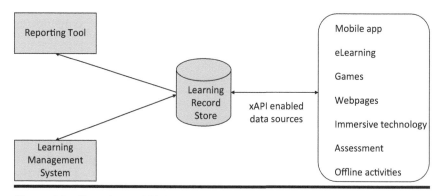

Figure 6.5   Experience API data sources.

The two most widely recognized data specifications are xAPI and IMS Caliper Analytics (Samuelsen et al., 2019). These specifications enable data to be exchanged between applications while integrating multiple sources of information in a central data store. They define metric profiles that utilize terms and concepts that software designers and developers can reference to describe everyday user interactions. Eradze et al. (2017) suggest that xAPI guidelines better support the integration with other data sources as they provide rules that can ensure consistency across different sources and interoperability across systems.

One of the most common data points collected is assessment information. Nouira, Cheniti-Belcadhi, and Braham (2018) carried out studies on the suitability of xAPI standards for assessment tracking and how this could be improved, suggesting that the field of research in assessment analytics is currently underexplored. They noted that the standards are suitable for tracking and storing learner data but may still have room for improvement when it comes to adding more detailed assessment records.

Nouira et al. (2018) explain that xAPI specifications can be considered in two parts: the format of the learning activity statement and the learning record itself. The learning activity statement is structured in a specific way that identifies a minimum of three attributes, such as actor, verb, and object, and can include additional attributes that are unique identifier, result, context, timestamp, stored, and authority (Glahn, 2013). The collection of this information enables consistent LA data to be imported from various sources (Figures 6.6).

Following are brief descriptions of the main xAPI attributes:

Actor: the actor, in this case, is typically the learner.
Verb: the verb refers to the activity that will be performed, that is, 'read' or 'listen.'
Object: the tool used to perform the activity, such as the 'PDF' or 'sound recording.'
Unique identifier: an identifier that is strictly unique and ensures each statement can be clearly identified.
Result: the result is the expected outcome of the activity, such as 'completed' or 'shared.'
Context: this provides broader information about an activity if relevant. For example, it may link to a parent or may be part of a group of activities.
Timestamp: the timestamp is a critical element that records the time that the event occurred.

Term	Description
Actor	The actor in learning analytics is typically the learner.
Verb	The verb refers to the activity that will be performed.
Object	The tool used to perform the activity.
Unique Identifier	An identifier that is unique and ensures each statement can be clearly identified.
Result	The result is the expected outcome of the activity.
Context	This provides broader information about an activity if relevant.
Timestamp	The timestamp records the time that the event occurred.
Stored	The stored element signifies when the data was transferred to the Learning Record Store.
Authority	The authority field validates who was responsible for recording the information.

Figure 6.6 Experience API table of attributes, information. Adapted from Gordon, Hayden, Johnson, and Smith (2020).

Stored: the stored element signifies when the data was transferred to the Learning Record Store.

Authority: the authority field validates who was responsible for recording the information.

In addition to this, when recording information that has come from outside the learning management system, it is advantageous to include further attributes, for example, expanding the *result* attribute to include score, success, duration, completion, and response, and also expanding the *context* attribute to include the type of assessment, the form of assessment and the assessment technique. This can provide more robust and useful assessment analytics (Nouira et al., 2018).

To further enhance these assessment-capturing possibilities, software applications such as portals, knowledge bases, and collaborative workspaces can offer data gathering opportunities using xAPI. When xAPI-enabled versions of these sorts of widely used business applications become available, learning designers will be able to seamlessly integrate learning activities into daily practice (Foreman, 2013). xAPI has a lot of potential, however, while there has been much development in this space, there is still ambiguity around some applications, terms, and best practices, meaning there is still work to be done in this space.

Adaptive Learning

Adaptive learning is a method that utilizes specific algorithms to tailor the interaction with the learner and deliver customized resources and activities to adapt to their unique requirements. Traditional training programs can be greatly enhanced with the use of personalized data and adaptive learning experiences that can fast track achievements and benefit the employee and the employer alike (Figures 6.7).

Intelligent adaptive learning systems are emerging quickly, though, in many ways, they are still in the experimental stages of development. These data-adaptive solutions enable differentiated learning experiences at a personalized level (Lin, Zhao, Liu, & Pu, 2020).

The level and type of course content can be dynamically adjusted to the individual learner's level of competency, which in turn accelerates the learner's achievements. The aim is to enhance an individual's learning journey with respect to the accuracy, speed, quality, and quantity of what they can learn. This can be leveraged to provide individuals and organizations with adaptive feedback as they progress through their learning journey.

In contrast to the development of traditional learning programs, according to Yuan (2019), an individualized adaptive learning model is much more robust as it mines data and uses sophisticated algorithms

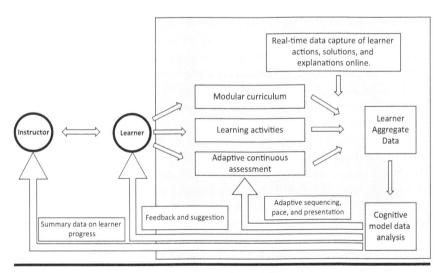

Figure 6.7   Adaptive learning system. Adapted from Hwang (2015).

to provide individualized learning paths. The mined data focuses on four main elements, which are:

Regularity

Finding relevant and regular information to help the learner grasp key knowledge points.

Individual Difference

An individual's behaviors and characteristics are analyzed and summarized into categories that generate pathways for differentiated learning experiences.

Skillfulness

Transferring the skills from a course allows the individual to solve the problems they encounter in real life.

Scalability

The way in which the model can be expanded and improved after the analysis and summary is extracted from the data-adaptive learning systems.

These elements inform personalized and accurate learning pathways that allow learners to build on existing knowledge and skills and make connections between a variety of learning experiences, while at the same time promising a huge increase in engagement and the fast-tracking of expertise (Antonio, Linda, & Jordi, 2018).

A simple example of workplace training that is usually not personalized in any way is that of compliance training. These typically dry and uninteresting courses are mandatory to undertake, and little deep learning actually occurs. Users tend to click through the content and check the boxes with as little thought and input as possible. There are two issues here, the first being that people are wasting time on clicking through content they are not absorbing or have already mastered, and the second being that to pass, they usually need to achieve a certain percentage of correct 'assessment.' Often this comes down to guesswork when using multiple-choice or similar assessment methods, not to mention the failed percentage could include some critical safety information that the user has not understood. Therefore, by using data to inform various touchpoints relating to different groups of users, the recommendations can be built into the design, and targeted information and assessments can be delivered to individuals.

Because learning has traditionally been linear and one-size-fits-all, the learner would continue to progress along a pre-determined learning path whether or not they have understood the information or mastered the skills. Adaptive learning, on the other hand, adjusts to the individual's needs and keeps lessons relevant and engaging. The most common components of adaptive learning are broken down to adaptive content, adaptive sequencing, and adaptive assessment (Brusilovsky & Millan, 2007), which are described as follows:

Adaptive Content

Content can be adapted by collecting various data points that indicate a learner's prior knowledge and preferences and replace parts of the content accordingly.

Adaptive Sequencing

Adaptive sequencing is the capacity to tailor the order in which learning materials are presented based on pre-determined pathways.

Adaptive Assessment

Adaptive assessment is altered to meet the learner's ability level. For example, if the learner performs well, they will be presented with a more difficult assessment. Likewise, if they performed poorly, they would be presented with an easier assessment.

These components, if programmed effectively, allow for a data-informed approach to personalized learning that updates and adapts content and assessment in real time and in the most suitable way for the individual.

Adaptive learning can take some time to establish, though it is usually worth the investment. Some common objectives for adaptive learning support systems include automated assessment, predictive analysis, provision of a variety of learning styles to users from different demographics, assessment of prior knowledge, staggered or streamlined progression dependent on mastery, learner ownership and self-mediation, feedback cycles, gathering of large-scale data to assist the instructor or designer, identification of individual learning styles, and an indication when intervention may be required (Pugliese, 2016).

Overall, the organization and its employees benefit as adaptive learning reduces the need for retraining while at the same time increasing engagement, efficacy, and the performance of employees.

Barriers to Adoption

When it comes to LA in the workplace, there are several barriers to adoption such as lack of understanding, poor implementation, competing workloads and priorities, ongoing maintenance, as well as genuine instances where LA may not yield strong enough returns on investment for particular companies.

The degree of adoption within organizations varies widely, and unfortunately, in many cases, it is even non-existent. Generally, the interest in LA in the workplace is considered relatively low because much of workplace learning is unstructured and informal, and it is therefore regarded as difficult to measure. Organizational learning is often ad hoc and driven by the need to solve problems or pursue personal goals and therefore lacks pedagogical design and structure (Ruiz-Calleja et al., 2019). However, learning that occurs digitally, mainly through learning management systems, is far more easily tracked and measured.

One of the most significant limitations of utilizing LA in the workplace is poor implementation. Change management approaches suggest that a critical step to implementing LA is to align it to company strategy. However, a study carried out by Macfadyen and Dawson (2012) revealed that when companies who were implementing LA were going through the technical selection process, the committee responsible gradually diverted their attention from the strategy to technical questions around the ease of data migration. While technical suitability is essential, in the absence of pedagogical vision and alignment to company goals, the likelihood that LA data will catalyze organizational improvement neutralizes (Macfadyen & Dawson, 2012).

Another limitation to adoption concerns the current workload and the effort it takes to implement and learn how to utilize the best new systems (Macfadyen & Dawson, 2012). Staff may feel it is an extra burden on them and resist the change, or they may have concerns that stem from a lack of understanding about what the technology is capable of and how they would benefit from it in practice. Also, because the adoption of LA in the workplace is not a set-and-forget activity, implementations can fail. LA is something that needs to be maintained, regularly assessed, and most importantly, it needs to inform the action taken after the data analysis has occurred.

Finally, a genuine barrier to adoption in some instances is that certain companies may not get a quality return on their investment. Dawson et al. (2015) raise the question that the instructional practices guiding learning in the workplace may not actually lend themselves to the same theoretical assumptions formed within formal learning environments. They claim it is undoubtedly true that all workplaces are different, and there may be companies that do not benefit from implementing LA (particularly if they are smaller businesses or seasonal companies with higher turnover rates).

There have also been studies that suggest there is little to no improvement to learning outcomes after the implementation of LA. Viberg, Hatakka, Bälter, and Mavroudi (2018) carried out recent studies that revealed LA had done little to improve learning outcomes in universities. A 2018 analysis on 252 papers on LA in higher education revealed that LA brought about as little as nine percent improvement. Still, despite the findings, this may not be a holistic representation. While there is a claim for LA to have a lot of potential to improve learning outcomes, the field and associated technologies are still relatively immature. The design and application in many cases may have significant room for improvement. Noting most importantly that LA will only bear the fruits of the actions taken after gathering and assessing the relevant data.

Privacy and Ethics

Privacy and ethics are somewhat controversial subjects that lack definitive guidelines around the implementation of LA in the workplace. Gathering and storing data have been debated topics in various areas when it comes to consent, access, storage, sharing, and use of information. However, there are common guidelines and expectations when utilizing personal data. These should be given serious consideration in the design and maintenance of LA and any other data analytics in the workplace.

The privacy and confidentiality of data should be ensured and not mistreated by the neglect of appropriate company policies or the lack of adherence to them. As a result of previous leaks of learner's personal details regarding achievements, assessments, and personally identifiable information, this has led to the call for a conceptual de-identification framework to prevent information being uncovered that links to an individual (Khalil & Ebner, 2016).

There is much professional and public debate around the ethics of data collection, including problems with algorithms, the risks of biases, and the potential of incorrectly predicting someone's behavior to their detriment (i.e., supplying insufficient or ill-fitting learning experiences as a result of data assumptions). Quality analytics is dependent on trusting the algorithms and the design of the intent behind the LA tools (Klein, Lester, Rangwala, & Johri, 2019). Studies carried out by Klein et al. (2019) note that when instructors were provided access to prior student performance data, this might have inadvertently influenced the assessment of current performances and increased the potential for bias.

While the extraction and analysis of learner data can provide useful insights, it can clearly create concern about privacy and ethical implications. Andergassen, Mödritscher, and Neumann (2014) suggest using an ethical framework that defines how data is captured and stored and that user consent should be acquired with an opt-out facility available. They outline six principles which are (Andergassen et al., 2014):

1. LA should function as a moral practice.
2. Learners should be considered agents.
3. Performance data collected should be considered temporal, dynamic constructs.
4. Achievement should be seen as multidimensional.
5. There should be transparency around data usage.
6. LA is used to better understand and develop learning outcomes.

It is also worth considering that because the data collected from learning management systems may present an incomplete picture and is encouraged to include data from multiple sources, the inclusion of such external data may heighten the risks associated with privacy and ethics (Olivier, 2020). Therefore, because learning is increasingly digital and data-driven, the issues around ethics and privacy are significant. While there are emerging frameworks to manage such concerns, there is still much work to do for consistency and clarity around these issues. Accountability, transparency, and regulatory frameworks will be essential elements in the future for ethical LA (Prinsloo & Slade, 2017).

Conclusion

With a continuous improvement mindset, LA can provide value by leveraging analytical insights that can breed responsible, agile learning environments. There are several strategies to help organizations get started with implementing LA. These include clearly defining objectives, developing strategy, adopting agreed-upon standards such as the xAPI specifications (Webb, 2019), and linking data from multiple sources to business activities such as KPIs, resulting in substantial opportunities for organizations to improve continuously. Providing learning experiences is not enough when the option is available to measure and evaluate training programs. Organizations that incorporate analytical capability can monitor, measure, and manage learning data, generating actionable insights and the potential for improved learning experiences and achievements across the company.

While LA is growing in popularity and may be a significant investment for some companies, they must also ensure the return on investment will be worthwhile, as there are some negative implications of LA integration, such as the abovementioned barriers to adoption and the privacy and ethical risks associated with data collection.

Critical Thinking Questions

1   In what ways can workplace learning programs be enhanced through the use of learning analytics?
2   Standards such as xAPI are used to allow consistency between various data sources. Why is this necessary?
3   When collecting data relating to individuals, what privacy and ethical considerations should be taken into account? What steps should be taken to ensure appropriate permission is obtained?
4   Adaptive learning is increasing in popularity for its ability to provide personalized learning opportunities that are adapted to the user at a specific point in time. What are the potential drawbacks of utilizing this technology?

5   Before implementing learning analytics into the workplace, planning should take place to determine objectives. Why is it important to decide on objectives before implementation?

References

Andergassen, M., Mödritscher, F., & Neumann, G. (2014). Practice and repetition during exam preparation in blended learning courses: Correlations with learning results. *Journal of Learning Analytics, 1*(1), 48–74. DOI:10.18608/jla.2014.11.4

Antonio, B., Linda, C., & Jordi, A. (2018). Personalization in educational technology: The absence of underlying pedagogies. *International Journal of Educational Technology in Higher Education, 15*(1), 1–17. DOI:10.1186/s41239-018-0095-0

Association for Computing Machinery. (2011). *Proceedings of the 1st International Conference on Learning Analytics and Knowledge. 1st International Conference on Learning Analytics and Knowledge*, Banff, Alberta, Canada.

Bersin, J. (2013). How corporate learning drives competitive advantage. *Forbes.* Retrieved from https://www.forbes.com/sites/joshbersin/2013/03/20/how-corporate-learning-drives-competitive-advantage/?sh=2d32542f17ad

Brusilovsky, P., & Millan, E. (2007). User models for adaptive hypermedia and adaptive educational systems. In P. Brusilovsky, A. Kobsa, & W. Nejdl (Eds.), *The adaptive web* (pp. 3–53). Berlin, Germany: Springer.

Dawson, S., Mirriahi, N., & Gasevic, D. (2015). Importance of theory in learning analytics informal and workplace settings. *Journal of Learning Analytics, 2*(2), 1–4. DOI:10.18608/jla.2015.22.1

Drachsler, H., Bogers, T., Vuorikari, R., Verbert, K., Duval, E., Manouselis, E. … Wolpers, M. (2010). Issues and considerations regarding sharable data sets for recommender systems in technology-enhanced learning. *Elsevier Procedia Computer Science, 1*(2), 2849–2858. DOI:10.1016/j.procs.2010.08.010

Eradze, M., Rodriguez Triana, M. J., & Laanpere, M. (2017). *How to aggregate lesson observation data into learning analytics datasets?* In *Joint Proceedings of the 6th Multimodal Learning Analytics (MMLA) Workshop and the 2nd Cross-LAK Workshop co-located with 7th International Learning Analytics and Knowledge Conference (LAK 2017)* (Vol. *1828*, No. CONF, pp. 74–81). Columbia, Canada: CEUR.

Foreman, S. (2013). *The xAPI and the LMS: What does the future hold?* Learning Solutions. Retrieved from https://learningsolutionsmag.com/articles/1271/the-xapi-and-the-lms-what-does-the-future-hold

García-Peñalvo, F. J. (2020). Learning analytics as a breakthrough in educational improvement. In D. Burgos (Eds.), *Radical solutions and learning analytics* (pp. 1–15). Springer. DOI:10.1007/978-981-15-4526-9_1

Glahn, C. (2013). *Using the ADL experience API for mobile learning, sensing, informing, encouraging, orchestrating.* In *2013 Seventh International Conference on Next Generation Mobile Apps, Services and Technologies* (pp. 268–273). IEEE. DOI:10.1109/NGMAST.2013.55

Gordon, J., Hayden, T., Johnson, A., & Smith, B. (2020). Total learning architecture 2019 report. *Advanced Distributed Learning Initiative.*

Greller, W., & Drachsler, H. (2012). Translating learning into numbers: A generic framework for learning analytics. *Journal of Educational Technology & Society, 15*(3), 42–57.

Hwang, S. (2015). *Adaptive learning.* Blended Learnings. Retrieved April 21 2021, from https://medium.com/blended-learnings/adaptive-learning-e52d53413b3b

Ifenthaler, D. (2020). Change management for learning analytics. In N. Pinkwart & S. Liu (Eds.), *Artificial intelligence supported educational technologies* (pp. 261–272). Springer. DOI:10.1007/978-3-030-41099-5_15

Khalil, M., & Ebner, M. (2016). De-identification in learning analytics. *Learning Analytics, 3*(1), 129–138. DOI:10.18608/jla.2016.31.8

Klein, C., Lester, J., Rangwala, H., & Johri, A. (2019). Technological barriers and incentives to learning analytics adoption in higher education: Insights from users. *Journal of Computing in Higher Education, 31*(3), 604–625. DOI:10.1007/s12528-019-09210-5

Lin, J., Zhao, Y., Liu, C., & Pu, H. (2020). *Personalized learning service based on big data for education.* In *2020 IEEE 2nd International Conference on Computer Science and Educational Informatization (CSEI)* (pp. 235–238). IEEE.

Macfadyen, L. P., & Dawson, S. (2012). Numbers are not enough. Why e-learning analytics failed to inform an institutional strategic plan. *Educational Technology & Society, 15*(3), 149–163.

Nitu, M., Dascalu, M. I., Lazarou, E., Trifan, E. L., & Bodea, C. N. (2018). *Learning analytics in an e-testing application: Premises and conceptual modelling.* In *The International Scientific Conference e-Learning and Software for Education* (Vol. *2*, pp. 239–246). DOI:10.12753/2066-026X-18-103

Nouira, A., Cheniti-Belcadhi, L., & Braham, R. (2018). An enhanced xAPI data model supporting assessment analytics. *Procedia Computer Science, 126*, 566–575. DOI:10.1016/j.procs.2018.07.291

Olivier, J. (2020). Research ethics guidelines for personalized learning and teaching through big data. In D. Burgos (Ed.), *Radical solutions and learning analytics* (pp. 37–55). Springer. DOI:10.1007/978-981-15-4526-9_3

Peña-Ayala, A., Cárdenas-Robledo, L. A., & Sossa, H. (2017). A landscape of learning analytics: An exercise to highlight the nature of an emergent field.

In A. Peña-Ayala (Ed.), *Learning analytics: Fundaments, applications, and trends* (pp. 65–112). Springer. DOI:10.1007/978-3-319-52977-6_3

Prinsloo, P., & Slade, S. (2017). Ethics and learning analytics: Charting the (un) charted. In C. Lang, G. Siemens, A. Wise, & D. Gasevic (Eds.), *Handbook of learning analytics* (pp. 49–57). SoLAR. DOI:10.18608/hla17.004

Pugliese, L. (2016). *Adaptive learning systems: Surviving the storm.* Colorado, USA: Educause Review.

Reffay, C., & Chanier, T. (2003, June). *How social network analysis can help to measure cohesion in collaborative distance learning [Paper presentation], International Conference on Computer Supported Collaborative Learning,* Bergen, Norway.

Ruiz-Calleja, A., Dennerlein, S., Kowald, D., Theiler, D., Lex, E., & Ley, T. (2019). An infrastructure for workplace learning analytics: Tracing knowledge creation with the social semantic server. *Journal of Learning Analytics, 6*(2), 120–139. DOI:10.18608/jla.2019.62.9

Samuelsen, J., Chen, W., & Wasson, B. (2019). Integrating multiple data sources for learning analytics—review of literature. *Research and Practice in Technology Enhanced Learning, 14*(1), 1–20. DOI:10.1186/s41039-019-0105-4

Secretan, J., Wild, F., & Guest, W. (2019). *Learning analytics in augmented reality: blueprint for an AR/xAPI framework. 2019 IEEE International Conference on Engineering, Technology and Education (TALE), Engineering, Technology and Education (TALE), 2019 IEEE International Conference On* (pp. 1–6). doi:10.1109/TALE48000.2019.9225931

SoLAR. (n.d.). *What is learning analytics.* SoLAR Research. Retrieved from https://www.solaresearch.org/about/what-is-learning-analytics/

Viberg, O., Hatakka, M., Bälter, O., & Mavroudi, A. (2018). The current landscape of learning analytics in higher education. *Computers in Human Behavior, 89,* 98–110. DOI:10.1016/j.chb.2018.07.027

Webb, L., (2019). *This is the future of learning analytics.* Training Journal. Retrieved from https://www.trainingjournal.com/articles/features/future-learning-analytics

Williamson, J. (2014). *An overview of learning analytics.* UCLA Office of Information Technology. Wikihub.berkeley.edu.

Yuan, X. (2019). *Model and implementation of personalized adaptive learning and analysis technology based on large data.* In *2019 International Conference on Artificial Intelligence and Advanced Manufacturing (AIAM)* (pp. 202–205). IEEE.

Chapter 7

Immersive Technologies for Workplace Learning

As technological trends point firmly toward the use of advanced simulations, immersive technologies are making a mark on the educational landscape. Because of their ability to bring the user into a sensory environment, the impact on learning is usually significant in terms of engagement, context, and motivation. While there is a considerable way to go in terms of widespread adoption, affordability, and seamless technological experiences, the use of immersive technologies in the workplace is growing slowly but steadily, with the potential for expansion on the horizon. This chapter outlines some of the benefits for workplace learning, the implementation of immersive technologies, measuring the impact on learning and development, meaningful assessment, and some of the common challenges involved with including immersive technologies in workplace learning.

The term immersive technology is used to describe devices and applications that simulate a virtual world, or characteristics of such, in which a user can feel immersed in their environment. The inclusion of sensory stimulation enhances the 'real' feeling, allowing the user to participate in ways beyond what they do in their regular, physical world.

This chapter will examine how virtual reality (VR) and augmented reality (AR) can be used to enhance workplace learning. The first thing to clarify is that VR and AR are not interchangeable terms. VR

DOI: 10.1201/9781003149132-8

is a three-dimensional, fully simulated environment that emulates real-world experiences or acts as an imaginary world. These virtual environments usually use a VR headset to project the experience and stimulate a variety of senses, predominantly visual, but also auditory, olfactory, haptic, and taste (Chandrasekera & Yoon, 2018). In comparison, AR is an overlay of virtual elements onto the user's real physical environment. It is considered a hybrid of physical and virtual realities (Chandrasekera & Yoon, 2018). Scavarelli (2020) describes the differences between VR and AR as follows: "*VR is an artificial environment in which a computer provides sensory stimuli that can be manipulated by one's actions. AR uses virtual objects that are superimposed into the real world, supplementing reality rather than replacing it.*" So, while there can be similarities and overlaps between VR and AR, they are two distinctly different technologies (Figure 7.1).

Without a doubt, these technologies will change the workplace as we know it, allowing workers to experience and achieve things that may otherwise be beyond our collective imaginations. So, let's consider some of the advantages of incorporating these tools into workplace training.

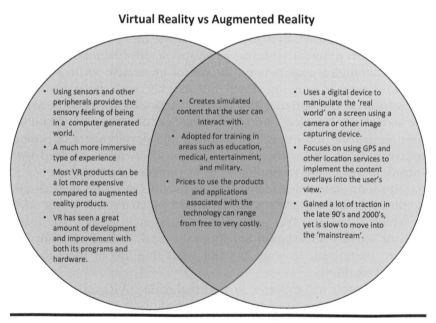

Figure 7.1   Virtual reality vs augmented reality. Adapted from De Falco (2015).

The Benefits of Using Immersive Technologies for Workplace Training

Many studies have examined the use of immersive technologies for learning and have revealed benefits in a variety of industries such as medicine, military, and higher education (Rogers et al., 2020; Ahir, Govani, Gajera & Shah, 2020; Awoke et al., 2021). These benefits include examples such as risk reduction, reduced time taken to train staff, increased contextualization, cost savings, emotional responses, and memory retention.

Risk Reduction

Learners can engage with different types of training experiences within VR and AR environments to make mistakes without real-world consequences. As risks are minimized or eliminated, they can practice their skills in the virtual environment and increase their confidence in carrying out the task, so it can then be performed in the real world. This can be particularly useful when solving problems or implementing new solutions, as workers can test possible processes without the risk of adverse consequences (Gabajova et al. 2019) should the experiment not achieve the desired results.

Workers can experience simulated situations, such as an operating theatre in which a training surgeon can perform simulated openheart surgery without risking a patient's life (Newman, 2016). Or they might experience the production of a machine that allows for trial and error without the risk of damaging equipment or losing parts (Gabajova et al., 2019). These types of no-risk hands-on experiences can significantly streamline the learning process.

Time to Train

It has long been known that 'learning by doing' increases knowledge retention (Aldrich, 2005), which is proven in studies such as the experiments performed by Ekstrand et al. (2018) on the use of VR in neuroanatomy training. This study revealed that the integration of interactive reality might have significantly helped improve knowledge attainment and retention and reduce time to mastery, while at the same time, increasing motivation.

Another example is the Walmart training module called 'The Pickup Tower,' in which over a million associates were trained using

VR, which reduced the training time from 8 hours to 15 minutes (Bailenson, 2020). This demonstrates when these types of training plans are implemented effectively, they can result in enormous time savings, and in turn, cost reductions for the company.

Cost Savings

While there are, of course, costs involved in setting up and maintaining simulated training environments for the workplace, there are also significant cost cuts in terms of hiring instructors, facilities, and physical equipment for the hands-on training.

However, the most significant cost-saving comes from the reduction in employee time spent training, practicing, and making errors. There is also the cost of secondary workers involved in training, such as supervising peers. These employees would no longer need to be removed from their role to shadow the learner while they master a skill, and instead, they can continue work on their primary tasks and provide support should it be required (Gabajova, 2019).

However, at the same time, there can be a significant outlay for equipment and applications to get an immersive technology training program started (these expenses are discussed below) and further costs for ongoing maintenance, updates, and support (Figure 7.2).

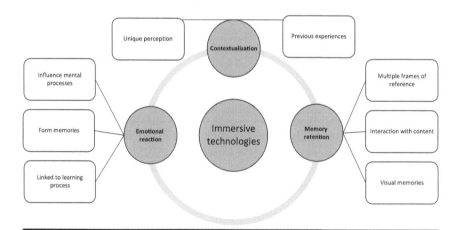

Figure 7.2 Immersive technology impact on learning.

Contextualization

According to Surya & Putri (2017), contextual learning emphasizes the entire process of an individual's involvement in what is being learned and how they relate that to real-life situations and apply it to their own lives. This type of learning requires an empowering approach, allowing workers to construct knowledge in their own minds rather than merely memorizing instructions or facts (Crawford, 2001). When learning occurs, the mind naturally seeks meaning in the context of the learner's world and their previous experiences. New information is absorbed in a way that makes sense to the individual and their unique perception at that point in time. With this in mind, it makes sense to utilize immersive technology for learning as the simulated experience aligns closely with the real-life context of how it should be applied. Scavarelli et al. (2020) explain that contextual learning allows new knowledge and skills to be transferred more easily when memory recall is closely associated with the environment. In VR/AR, the environment can feel realistic, thus creating real memories of completing activities rather than relying on theoretical or abstract ideas.

Emotional Reaction

At a fundamental level, cognitive activity is motivated by basic emotional needs that evaluate new information first of all, in terms of survival, and secondarily to serve the processes of memory and learning (Tyng, Amin, Saad, & Malik. 2017). Emotional responses are central to forming memories (McGaugh, 2003). They influence mental processes, including attention, perception, problem solving, memory, and reasoning, which are all linked to the learning process (Tyng et al., 2017).

While emotional theory and research are complex, and in many cases, raise more questions than answers, it is safe to say that we know there is evidence of emotional experiences driving attention, motivation, learning, and memory (McGaugh, 2003), and this is what drives memory storage. Therefore, by immersing in real-life training experiences, it is more likely to garner emotion than learning through non-immersive, passive styles of instruction.

Memory Retention

Naturally, most people won't make significant memory connections when they read or hear about something compared to experiencing it for themselves. It is the improved immersion in learning that is beneficial and the opportunity to view multiple frames of reference (Scavarelli et al. 2020), which gives the learner a deeper understanding of how things work. As the participant touches and moves objects, pulls things apart, and examines systems, they gain first-hand experience, allowing them to form meaningful memories that are second only to the real-life activity.

The vividness with which the interaction is communicated in a VR environment, including the visual representations, enhances the cognitive responses. Cho (2018) recommends to VR content creators that this can be further enhanced by increasing spatial presence and high resolution.

Implementing VR/AR Learning in the Workplace

While VR and AR technologies have been around for decades, in various levels of sophistication and adoption, it can be suggested that these technologies are relatively still in their infancy (Ekstrand et al., 2018). Some companies have matured virtual systems throughout their organizations and embedded them into their training programs, while others may not have even considered the opportunities that come with immersive technology (Figure 7.3).

Implementing new technologies shouldn't be done for the sake of change but should be considered carefully in light of the needs of the business, its customers, and its workforce. If immersive technologies are proven to provide improved learning experiences in a shorter time and with more motivated participants, then consider what learning needs can be addressed and how this could be implemented. These are essential things to contemplate in the planning phase for any new training program, particularly one that involves high levels

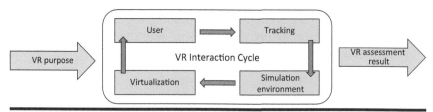

Figure 7.3 Immersive technology interaction cycle. Adapted from Otto, Lampen, Agethen, Langohr, Zachmann, & Rukzio (2019).

of investment and commitment. It is also worth remembering that it takes time to figure out how to design optimal systems and apply them effectively to training. Fully understanding and appreciating the ethical considerations, optimization, potential barriers, and cultural effects is an iterative process that takes time. Therefore, while training with these technologies is suitable for most industries and workplaces, particularly if starting with standard training programs like those for compliance, safety, soft skills, and onboarding, it is helpful to start small and monitor results (Gabajova, et al. 2019).

However, while the uptake in many general areas of workplace training may not yet be widespread, several vital industries utilize sophisticated immersive technologies for training and have been heavily investing in this for some time. According to Barad (2018), organizations such as NASA were responsible for the original development of VR to facilitate training for their space exploration programs, contrary to a common belief that VR was developed for the gaming world. More recently, industries have made significant breakthroughs with advanced simulation programs, examples are outlined by Scavarelli et al. (2020) as flight simulation in the avionics industry, surgery training in the field of medicine, and military training for special forces.

A popular example of a military training program is the Virtual Battlespace (VB) developed by Bohemia Interactive. For over 20 years, Bohemia Interactive has developed military-style games and more serious training solutions for the armed forces worldwide. VB is the flagship product designed as a complex simulation software and is currently used in over 50 countries to train hundreds of thousands of soldiers (Bohemia Interactive Australia Pty Ltd, 2012). Using a 'whole earth' virtual desktop simulation, military training scenarios can be constructed for almost any imaginable scene. Terrains can be generated and edited to recreate real-life terrain or adjusted to suit more complex training requirements. This facilitates cognitive learning based on setting up a unique and specific situation where the soldier needs to achieve the set goals using the assets at hand. It is essentially like rehearsing real-life possibilities before they happen, so when a similar instance occurs, the soldier feels more mentally prepared.

Many companies, both established and emerging, are developing ground-breaking training solutions using immersive technologies, and it is a fascinating area to watch. Advances continue to be made in artificial intelligence support, useful learning analytics, just-in-time training, and spreading knowledge about what immersive technology training can achieve. These advancements lead to the conclusion that the critical question isn't 'if' immersive technologies can enhance training, but 'in what ways' and 'to what degree' the training can be enhanced.

Measuring the Impact of Immersive Training Technologies

Performance measurement is an integral part of any training program, and evaluating the impact of immersive technologies provides quality data that can uncover the success or gaps in training. While there is little published research around direct comparisons of training programs using VR or AR compared to those that don't use these tools, it is an area that has huge potential to be explored in the future.

However, when it comes to measuring the training impact, it is understood that learning data can be effectively collected and measured through the use of immersive technologies (Ekstrand et al., 2018). Every action a learner takes which uses simulation technology can be captured, for example, simple information such as usage data (who completed the course, how long it took when they completed it), can be collected along with less common examples such as physical performance indicators (eye-tracking, body movements, time to act), which demonstrate how a learner would potentially function with the activity in the real world. These indicators are much less likely to be available without the use of immersive technologies.

The additional metrics available when using simulations also open up further abilities to analyze and improve training. Development is taking place in the area of data capture for learning analytics, including one such study carried out by Secretan, Wild, and Guest (2019) where they propose a model that can implement an xAPI framework (eLearning specifications that makes it possible to collect data on a range of learning experiences in both online and offline environments), using recommended statements over an existing AR training program. Examples of VR/AR style actions that can be written into xAPI statements include 'locate the tool,' 'read the text,' or 'press the button.' These actions can be recorded in a central or decentralized analytics storage endpoint (Secretan, Wild & Guest, 2019).

However, it is worth noting that a single statement is unlikely to describe the full competency, as these would require sequences of statements that make up the activities. Secretan, Wild, & Guest (2019) claim that by implementing such statements properly, a good VR/AR learning analytics system can form successful statement sequences that insert 'completed' along with 'passed' or 'failed' at the end of the statement. (One example of this in action can be found in the Open-Source project LearningLocker, where the learning record store acts as a streaming database for the embedded xAPI statements (Learning Pool, n.d.)).

Overall, because VR and AR training can be integrated directly within the learning management system, it becomes relatively easy to analyze data and show the investment value. Immersive technologies can generate multiple data points aligned to company strategies and business goals, thus measuring the importance of training and demonstrating value to stakeholders.

Meaningful Assessment through Immersive Technology

Assessment is an integral part of all training as it provides feedback to the learner and allows the instructor to follow up accordingly. VR and AR assessment methods can capture performance data in several ways that can provide in-depth analysis of learning progression. These methods can include self-validation, instructor observation, or recorded completion of performance criteria within the system (Secretan, Wild & Guest, 2019). Assessment metrics can be widely varied and include typical pass/fail activities, as well as the methods mentioned above such as time to completion, eye tracking, body movements, and time to act.

However, interaction with VR/AR is part of a larger assessment picture. Progression can be monitored by incorporating a variety of assessment points such as user demographics, information about the learner's prior knowledge, experience with the digital tools, and the learner's attitude toward the process (Christopoulos, Pellas & Laakso 2020). These broader data collection methods encapsulate a more well-rounded picture of learner competency and lead to targeted feedback and interventions.

Assessment results from immersive technologies can also be fed into personalized adaptive learning techniques. However, while immersive technology that provides real-time feedback may not be widely and readily available, with the rate at which developments are advancing, it will make a likely appearance in the not-too-distant future. One such example of advancements being made in this space is a study carried out by Iqbal, Mangina, and Campbell (2019). They explored an early-stage prototype designed to provide feedback within an AR application. The approach was to enhance the learning process by acting out scenarios in real-time while being led by an intelligent guide. Iqbal, Mangina, and Campbell (2019) claim that the learning process was enhanced due to the intelligent program's ability to intervene and provide assistance when necessary rather than wait for post-participation feedback. There are a number of similar, basic programs emerging, though the more widespread inclusion and adoption of these programs may require further progress.

Therefore, for the time being, it is well worth the efforts to include assessment activities using immersive technology while at the same time ensuring that it makes up part of a broader range of activities that depict a user's level of competency.

Common Challenges

While VR and AR technologies have tremendous potential, they are still far from being seamless, one-size-fits-all solutions for workplace training. Scavarelli et al. (2020) note that there is strong evidence to suggest that VR-based instruction positively enhances learning experiences. However, they also point out that a challenge to its integration includes determining how to best utilize the technology for training. In the workplace, there appears to be a limited ability to appropriately target learning outcomes for VR and AR and effectively map them to workplace competencies without being distracted by the novelty of the technologies (Chandrasekera & Yoon, 2018). In addition to this, Christopoulos (2020) points out that there is no distinct framework for collecting and interpreting data at this stage, nor are there approved guidelines that can be used for standardization across the industry.

Therefore, while immersive technologies show potential for learning and development in the workplace, there are legitimate reasons for the relatively limited uptake to date. Besides the lack of standards and frameworks to lay the foundations for successful integration,

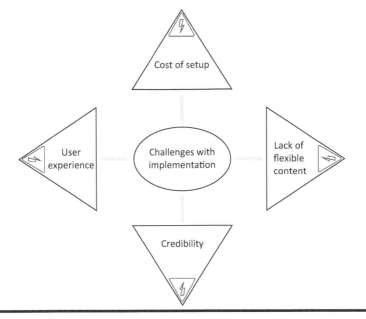

Figure 7.4   Challenges with implementing immersive technology programs in the workplace.

there are also other issues such as the perceived cost of setup, lack of relevant content, problems with user experience, and possible lack of educational credibility (Figure 7.4).

The Perceived Cost of Setup

Purchasing VR equipment is not only costly but there is also little understanding of the longevity of the tools due to the rapid advancement of the technology, which may leave some devices and applications redundant. Because it is still costly for VR companies to produce hardware and software, there is little room for prices to be dropped. In addition to this, there are support systems that need investment, such as gaming-level processors and high-speed, reliable Wi-Fi connectivity, further contributing to the costs.

On the other hand, AR is much easier to include using existing devices such as Smartphones and can be quite cost-effective to trial various programs. The actual expense in this area is when customized training programs are developed, which can be quite time-intensive and expensive.

Lack of Flexible Content

Immersive learning content is being introduced to the market continuously, but there is inconsistency with quality, relevance, and intended learning outcomes. While a learning and development professional may be able to source some quality content, if they are unable to source content for an extensive range of training programs for their organization, it may not be worth the investment in the hardware to begin with. AR programs may be available but don't have the flexibility of making changes unless costly development is undertaken. Also, because there is still a lack of technical standards in the VR and AR design spaces, the development process becomes cumbersome and costly.

Virtual Reality User Experience

The user experience can be mixed depending on the technology used, along with the supporting systems. Some VR headsets are tethered with cords, making the ability to move around limited or even dangerous. In contrast, those that aren't tethered may have slower response times, detracting from the visual user experience.

There is also the issue of 'cyber sickness' in which some users may feel disorientated, uncomfortable, or even nauseous and claustrophobic. It is also worth noting that the long-term effects of using VR have not been explored, meaning that we really don't know if any lasting side effects could include confusion, loss of balance, headaches, and other health complications.

Lack of Credibility for Training

VR and AR have gained reputations predominantly as gaming platforms and amusement-style experiences. When people think about AR, they are more likely to think of an application such as Pokémon Go. When thinking of VR, they are generally more likely to associate that with a war game than an educational program. While tech enthusiasts who are familiar with the capabilities can articulate the potential for training, the public majority may perceive it as more of a gimmick for the gaming world. To compound this problem, the expense of the technologies means the average person owns little or no immersive technology equipment and is therefore unaware of what it is capable of or what it actually does.

Overall, the challenges involved with integrating immersive technologies into workplace learning programs should be mitigated over time. As the field advances and technology improves, many of the limitations and challenges will be diminished.

Conclusion

Immersive technologies have significant potential to enhance learning in the workplace due to their ability to bring the user into a sensory environment and increase engagement, context, and motivation. These technologies have progressed over the past two decades and continue to make in-roads into improving learning experiences. There is further potential that may be realized once these technologies advance further and continue to expand the possibilities for inclusion in the workplace.

This chapter examined some of the benefits and limitations of including immersive technology in workplace learning. Considering benefits such as reduced risk, shorter time to train, and improved memory retention, and offsetting them with the potential challenges such as the cost of setup, limited flexible content, limits to user experience, and lack of credibility, there may be various degrees of interest and adoption across a variety of industries.

User perception is mainly mixed, though because of the general lack of experience with such technologies in the community, it is fair to say, as advancements are made, and the use of VR and AR become more commonplace, there may be further interest in utilizing these tools more expansively for workplace training. Therefore, while VR and AR are two distinctly different technologies, they can both immerse a learner into an environment of heightened sensory experience, and they both should undoubtedly have a place in learning and development in the future.

Critical Thinking Questions

1 Learning new things using immersive technologies can lead to an increase in contextualization. What does this mean for the learner, and how does it improve learning outcomes?

2 Some industries have invested heavily in training programs delivered through immersive technologies, including the fields

of medicine and the military. What other industries could benefit from extensive training experiences that utilize these technologies?

3 Training outcomes can be measured through the use of immersive technologies and learning analytics combined. What role do standards such as xAPI play in measuring these outcomes?

4 One of the challenges to implementing immersive technology training in the workplace is the perceived cost of the initial setup. How can this cost be offset within an organization?

References

Ahir, K., Govani, K., Gajera, R., & Shah, M. (2020). Application on virtual reality for enhanced education learning, military training, and sports. *Augmented Human Research*, *5*(1). DOI:10.1007/s41133-019-0025-2

Aldrich, C. (2005). *Learning by doing: A comprehensive guide to simulations, computer games, and pedagogy in e-learning and other educational experiences*. New York: Pfeiffer.

Awoke, A., Burbelo, H., Childs, E., Mohammad, F., Stevens, L., Rewkowski, N., & Manocha, D. (2021). *An overview of enhancing distance learning through augmented and virtual reality technologies*. Cornell University. Retrieved from https://arxiv.org/abs/2101.11000

Bailenson, J. (2020). *Is VR the future of corporate training? Harvard Business Review*. Retrieved from https://hbr.org/2020/09/is-vr-the-future-of-corporate-training

Barad, J. (2018, March 9). *Advanced surgical training with virtual reality [Video] YouTube*. Retrieved from https://www.youtube.com/watch?v=ue2m75G7Ci4

Bohemia Interactive Australia Pty Ltd. (2012). *White paper: VBS2 [White paper]*. Retrieved from https://bisimulations.com/sites/default/files/file_uploads/VBS2_Whitepaper.pdf

Chandrasekera, T., & Yoon, S. Y. (2018). Augmented reality, virtual reality and their effect on learning style in the creative design process. *Design and Technology Education*, *23*(1), 55–75.

Cho, Y. (2018). *How spatial presence in VR affects memory retention and motivation on second language learning: a comparison of desktop and immersive VR-based learning*. (Doctoral dissertation, Syracuse University). New York.

Christopoulos, A., Pellas, N., & Laakso, M. J. (2020). A learning analytics theoretical framework for STEM education virtual reality applications. *Education Sciences*, *10*(11), 317. DOI:10.3390/educsci10110317

Crawford, M. L. (2001). *Teaching contextually: Research, rationale, and techniques for improving student motivation and achievement in mathematics and science.* The University of Texas at Austin Charles A. Dana Center. Dana Center Mathematics Pathway. Retrieved from https://dcmathpathways.org/resources/teaching-contextually-research-rationale-and-techniques-improving-student-motivation-and

De Falco, T. (2015). *Augmented reality, virtual reality's older and more forgotten brother.* Revolution Tech. Retrieved April 16, 2021 from https://revolutiontechblog.wordpress.com/2015/12/09/augmented-reality-virtual-realitys-older-and-more-forgotten-brother/

Ekstrand, C., Jamal, A., Nguyen, R., Kudryk, A., Mann, J., & Mendez, I. (2018). Immersive and interactive virtual reality to improve learning and retention of neuroanatomy in medical students: A randomized controlled study. *CMAJ Open, 6*(1), 103–109. DOI:10.9778/cmajo.20170110

Gabajova, G., Furmannova, B., Medvecka, I., Grznar, P., Krajčovič, M., & Furmann, R. (2019). Virtual training application by use of augmented and virtual reality under university technology-enhanced learning in Slovakia. *Sustainability, 11*(23), 6677. DOI:10.3390/su11236677

Iqbal, M. Z., Mangina, E., & Campbell, A. G. (2019). *Exploring the use of augmented reality in a kinaesthetic learning application integrated with an intelligent virtual embodied agent.* In *2019 IEEE International Symposium on Mixed and Augmented Reality Adjunct (ISMAR-Adjunct)* (pp. 12–16). IEEE. DOI:10.1109/ISMAR-Adjunct.2019.00018

Learning Pool (n.d.) The world's most installed learning record store. *Learning Pool.* Retrieved April 17 2021, from https://learning-pool.com/solutions/learning-record-store-learning-locker/learning-locker-community-overview/

McGaugh, J. L. (2003). *Memory and emotion: The making of lasting memories.* New York: Columbia University Press.

Newman, D. (2016). Hyper-training and the future augmented reality workplace. *Forbes Magazine.* Retrieved from https://www.forbes.com/sites/danielnewman/2016/09/20/hyper-training-and-the-future-augmented-reality-workplace/

Otto, M., Lampen, E., Agethen, P., Langohr, M., Zachmann, G., & Rukzio, E. (2019). A virtual reality assembly assessment benchmark for measuring VR performance & limitations. *Procedia CIRP, 81*, 785–790. DOI:10.1016/j.procir.2019.03.195

Rogers, M. P., DeSantis, A. J., Janjua, H., Barry, T. M., & Kuo, P. C. (2020). The future surgical training paradigm: Virtual reality and machine learning in surgical education. *Surgery.* DOI:10.1016/j.surg.2020.09.040

Scavarelli, A., Arya, A., & Teather, R. J. (2020). Virtual reality and augmented reality in social learning spaces: A literature review. *Virtual Reality, 25*, 1–21. DOI:10.1007/s10055-020-00444-8

Secretan, J., Wild, F., & Guest, W. (2019). *Learning analytics in augmented reality: Blueprint for an AR/xAPI framework*. In *2019 IEEE International Conference on Engineering, Technology and Education (TALE)* (pp. 1–6). IEEE. DOI:10.1109/TALE48000.2019.9225931

Surya, E., & Putri, F. A. (2017). Improving mathematical problem-solving ability and self-confidence of high school students through contextual learning model. *Journal on Mathematics Education*, *8*(1), 85–94. DOI: 10.22342/jme.8.1.3324.85-94

Tyng, C. M., Amin, H. U., Saad, M. N. M., & Malik, A. S. (2017). The influences of emotion on learning and memory. *Frontiers in Psychology*, *8*, 1454. DOI:10.3389/fpsyg.2017.01454

Chapter 8

Emerging Trends for Digital Workplace Learning

Trends, as defined by Merriam-Webster (2021), are *"the general movements over time of a statistically detectable change,"* and in the case of digital learning trends, it is clear to see that the technology landscape is evolving quicker than ever before. These shifts have occurred for several reasons, as external impacts actively shape the world around us and drive the direction of learning technologies.

This chapter is divided into two sections. The first focuses on the driving forces behind digital trends such as the changes in workforce composition, the revised learning landscape, the digital economy, newly defined workplace roles, investment in technology, the need for innovation, and the disruption and decentralization of the workforce. The second section focuses on the digital trends themselves, such as artificial intelligence (A.I.), personalized learning, Comprehensive Learner Records (CLRs), mobile learning, microlearning, and Learning Experience Platforms (LXPs).

Driving Forces behind Digital Trends

There have been significant impacts on workplaces over the past few years (Figure 8.1), and the results have contributed to shaping the

DOI: 10.1201/9781003149132-9

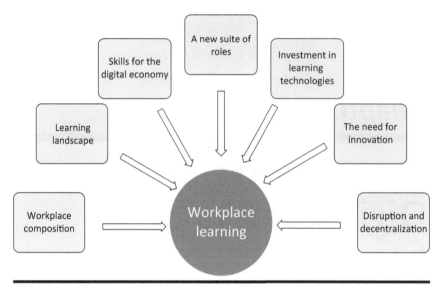

Figure 8.1 Driving forces behind trends in workplace learning.

digital learning trends we see today. Following, we examine several of these impacts.

Workforce Composition

As workplace trends continue to point in the direction of flexible organizations that are digitally connected and able to scale, reconfigure, and pivot to meet challenges, it is more apparent than ever before that the ability for workers to learn, reskill, and adapt is essential (Verhoef et al., 2019). As technologies advance and companies continue to grow and develop, workers' skills need to be updated to accommodate the revised and often more advanced skillsets.

According to a recent report by Deloitte (Schwartz, Hatfield, Jones, & Anderson, 2019), the three fundamental aspects of work that are rapidly changing are:

1. The workforce
2. The workplace
3. The work itself

The future-ready workforce is flexible, scalable, and made up of many types of workers worldwide. The changing workplace blends virtual and physical environments, collaborative tools, and personalized experiences that empower workers to be their best. The work itself is also evolving, as workers interact with technology, allow the automation of tasks, and explore new ways of working with digital technologies (Schwartz, Hatfield, Jones, & Anderson, 2019).

As a result of the COVID-19 pandemic, the need for businesses to adapt to these more modern ways of working has hastened. Organizations that thrive post-pandemic will be those that are flexible, borderless, and reconfigurable, nurturing talent and employee lifestyle. Because we have now seen how volatile the world can be and how changes occur, the culture of continuous learning and development is paramount. Organizations and individuals alike are reinventing themselves or finding new, suitable opportunities. The pandemic has forced a new way of life onto the workforce that will most probably never return to the way it was before 2020.

There had also been significant changes to workforce composition over the preceding decade that saw the rise of contractors and freelancers and the decrease in permanent, traditional-style employment. The effects of globalization and the gig economy allowed companies to retract and expand as required, sourcing the talent they need for the jobs required at the time.

A report released by McKinsey and Company suggests that because of the structural changes to employment landscapes, there is a dire need to equip their workers with the meta-skill of learning how to learn (Nielsen, Dotiwala, & Murray, 2020) as this enables self-direction. They go on to say that companies should be seizing learning and development initiatives with both hands and reimagining every aspect of how their workforce continuously learns (Nielsen, Dotiwala, & Murray, 2020).

During the pandemic, many workforces were entirely reliant on online approaches to learning. Social distancing prevented face-to-face training, which may have formed the foundations of a new normal for companies across the globe. Therefore, the ability for workers of all ages, backgrounds, and abilities to access and navigate online learning platforms and other digital technologies is more relevant than ever before.

The Revised Learning Landscape

Learning can no longer be considered an 'add-on' or optional extra in the workplace. Despite the pandemic, learning was already evolving as an essential building block for organizational performance, and because of the pandemic, this progress has accelerated.

According to Dean and Campbell (2020), the recent and rapid transition to online learning has revealed the value of alternative forms of integrated education. After the initial panic and experimentation settles, the purposeful design of learning in non-workplace settings requires proper thought and attention. Dean and Campbell (2020) claim that recent practice has demonstrated that work tasks can be effectively harnessed using digital methods. Because of this, traditional workplace learning can also be redesigned and accommodated.

Companies are discovering that learning is an effective business strategy that must be put on the agenda to develop sustainable workforces that are digitally literate and can continuously upskill and reskill to keep their business competitive into the future.

Skills for the Digital Economy

In 2016, the OECD produced a report on the New Skills for the Digital Economy, which responds to the requirement for enhanced ICT skills. They identify the following significant areas for change:

Generic Skills

Generic ICT skills are taking on increased importance globally, as jobs require taking on many different digital tasks. Basic, transferrable ICT skills enable workers to engage and contribute to digital working practices.

1. Specialist skills

On the other hand, specialist ICT skills involve expert knowledge and skills relating to a particular area. Workers with these skills take on specific functions and support those around them by leveraging one specific technology area.

2. Complementary skills

Complementary skills include a variety of skills that, when combined, become more significant than the individual skills on their own. Complementary ICT skills can contribute to accomplishing goals using the coordinated efforts of several individuals.

The OECD (2016) compares the demand and supply of ICT generic skills and links the data between the OECD Adult Competencies and their national Labour Force Surveys. The report presents evidence that the use of digital skills in the workplace is increasing significantly. As a result of specialist ICT roles, the impact on 'non-ICT' roles is that their use of technology and need for digital literacy skills has also increased (Spiezia, Koksal-Oudot, & Montagnier, 2016). Likewise, the World Economic Forum published an article by Gray (2017) outlining the need to develop a workforce with solid digital literacy skills. Both of these documents were produced pre-COVID-19, and these needs have only exacerbated. Gray (2017) suggests three critical ways for employers to develop digital literacy skills among their workforce:

1. Identify the required competencies and develop these skills throughout the workforce.
2. Uncover hidden talent in the workforce by regularly assessing skills (and encouraging knowledge sharing and collaboration).
3. Hire digital leaders who can bring new skills into the company and share their knowledge.

Companies that get this right, and develop the digital skills of their workforce, will not only increase their digital capabilities but also enable their workers and their business streams to bolster a variety of other hard and soft skills along the way. Their ability to execute these diverse skillsets will set these companies and individuals apart and pave the way for the future economy. Therefore, it is clear that the organizations that put digital literacy and ongoing education at the core of their business strategy will have an advantage – as will their employees.

A New Suite of Roles

The belief that a person has a job for life still exists in some industries, though in an increasingly large number of areas, this idea no longer prevails. This idea retired some time ago and has been cemented over the past decade. It is also true that many of the jobs for the next generation aren't likely to even exist today. While these uncertainties have been common knowledge for some time, they seem to be happening quicker and with more intensity than expected.

Job descriptions that last a lifetime may be a thing of the past, and people not only change roles an average of 12 times throughout their careers (U.S. Bureau of Labor Statistics, 2019) but are actually predicted to change industries several times throughout their working life. This doesn't necessarily indicate that workers start from scratch with every transition, but instead, they build on their skillsets. For example, an individual may enter the workplace as a nursing assistant before becoming a theatre nurse. They then move out of the hospital environment and travel as a pharmaceutical sales representative before returning to nursing, this time in aged care. In later years, they may decide to again move away from the physical exertion involved with nursing and transition into the clinical administration space. Perhaps in later years, they translate their skills to become a medical consultant for a software development company. This depicts the continuous transition and fluid nature of one's professional journey that is not wedded to a particular role or organization.

At the same time, when looking at today's organizational structures, there is a vast array of jobs that didn't exist a couple of decades ago. Take IT departments, for example (those who are part of general companies and not IT-based companies in their own right). Traditionally, there may have been a couple of support desk workers and a systems administrator, both reporting into finance because there seemed to be nowhere else for them to fit into the organizational structure. Now complex IT departments are featuring CIOs, CTOs, systems analysts, data architects, UX designers, developers, test managers, etc. This highlights the emergence of new roles that did not exist in previous times. Because of the variety and nature of newly created roles in the workplace, the need for continuous learning is more relevant than ever before and is one of the drivers of digital advancements.

Large-Scale Investment in Learning Technologies

Another driver of digitally enhanced learning in the workplace is the large-scale investment in learning technologies. These investments were originally more focused on the higher education environment, though they have expanded to workplace training and will continue to feature as their importance is further prioritized.

Markets and Markets (2020) claim organizations are increasingly making significant investments in workplace learning technologies for various reasons. They claim factors such as the increased adoption of digital learning, government initiatives for the growth of digital learning tools, and the rising significance of eLearning in corporate setups have led to such widespread investment. However, it is essential to note that while an increasing number of businesses realize that they need to have robust and ongoing learning programs in the workplace, they may find this to be a challenging scenario in terms of implementation, generational challenges, management concerns, and resistance to change (Delaney & D'Agostino, 2015).

Again, the COVID-19 pandemic has accelerated the need for digital workplace learning, and large corporations are responding to these requirements. This is good news for educational technology companies that can adapt and keep up with the emerging trends in this space.

However, it is not only the global pandemic that has brought this into focus. There is also the need for employers to develop their talent and remain competitive in the marketplace. A recent Forbes article pointed out that while we spend billions of dollars as a society on measuring the return on investment (ROI) of our financial assets, we still haven't applied even a proportional response to improving the ROI of our workforce (Shimkus, 2019). Shimkus (2019) also suggests that in today's world, skills are more important than capital and predicts that over the next 30 years, the winning and losing organizations will be determined by their ability to not only attract good talent but develop it accordingly.

Needless to say, the need for digital learning environments in the workplace is not likely to be something that will recede in value, and organizations across the globe are quickly investing in these technologies. The companies that are accepting and ready for these changes are also those who will be more likely to thrive in the era of disruption and decentralization.

The Need for Innovation

Innovation, which can be defined as activity that results in new or improved products, goods, and services through new methods (Dan Andrei, 2019), allows both individuals and companies to grow. Innovation is becoming a necessary skill for workers as it enables them to contribute to enhancing and improving business practice. The application of these skills produces ideas, systems, and concepts that are fresh and unique, and while most people are born with creative abilities, they may become diluted as they progress through adulthood. However, innovative capabilities can be reintroduced and reinforced with effective training, support, and practice.

According to Totterdill (2013), there should be two fundamental behaviors for people when they are working. The first is to complete their designated tasks in the best possible way, and the second is to draw on their own ideas and previous experience to improve business outcomes. Every individual has a wealth of knowledge, experience, and unique perspectives, and drawing on these personal qualities is often overlooked. Therefore, incorporating innovative education and innovative practice is a relatively easy way to leverage this potential. When workers are trained on how to think innovatively, they are likely to bring more of themselves to their role and actively participate in solving problems (Nakata, 2020).

While the traditional paradigm of workplace innovation focused on industry and associated technology, the more recent paradigm shift has gravitated toward an encompassing view of how technological innovation, social development, and scientific research work together (Chen Yin & Mei, 2018). This allows for workers to become engaged and empowered at all levels, and it leads to true, sustainable improvements.

Fostering innovative practices in the workplace takes positive leadership that can enable a culture shift toward creative thinking. However, it has been acknowledged that while there are many forward-thinking and creative leaders who inspire innovation, there are also many leaders who are not very innovative, or they don't have the room to express themselves and experiment with new ideas, systems, and concepts. Moreover, western culture often teaches us that leadership is displayed with certainty, which rules out the ability to experiment and experience failure (Wilson, 2013). Whereas trial and error and continuous improvement should be encouraged, and when contingency measures and guidelines are in place to ensure unnecessary risks are not taken, there are plenty of ways to practice and learn how to be innovative within safe environments. In addition to this, opportunities for reflection and allowing all worker's voices to be heard can lead to optimal results (Totterdill, 2013). Creating a safe and supportive environment conducive to developing creativity can open up new possibilities, and this is made particularly evident through the use of digital tools such as virtual reality. By making creativity the norm and allowing attempts that may end in initial failure, the scope for what a business can achieve is expanded.

Disruption and Decentralization

The National Governors Association for Best Practice (NGA Center) produced a report that discussed the workplace disruptions that occurred before the COVID-19 outbreak and identified three major economic paradigm shifts that ensued. These were: (1) Acceleration of job creation and elimination. (2) The dramatic shift in required skills as existing roles were redefined. (3) Increased participation in the on-demand workforce as more individuals became reliant on self-employed, freelance, or entrepreneurial work (Ash and Rahn, 2020). In addition to this, it noted that the workforce is in an acute need of rapid reskilling and that working from home arrangements have exposed a significant lack in preparedness for 21st century ways of working (Ash and Rahn, 2020).

This global disruption to business has been like nothing experienced in our lifetimes, forcing the decentralization of a significant proportion of workplaces across the world. This has forced organizations to rapidly review and revise their digital architecture, their service offerings, and in many cases, the entire operations of their businesses. The process of decentralizing a company is complex, to say the least, though contingency planning may help to avoid further disruption should another crisis strike. Successful decentralization requires a robust infrastructure and supportive culture and can have its benefits, though workers need to be accountable, autonomous, agile, and able, highlighting the need for ongoing distance learning opportunities. However, such disruption and decentralization have ultimately accelerated the speed at which the following trends advance in the marketplace.

Digital Learning Trends in the Workplace

As a result of the workplace's developments mentioned above, the following emerging trends are gaining momentum and are worth thoughtful evaluation. Most have been around for some time and have increased in capability and offering, but all are worth consideration.

Artificial Intelligence

A.I. incorporates human-like thinking with rational action (Russell & Norvig, 2014) and can describe computer technologies that can imitate human cognitive functions such as problem-solving and complex learning (Spector & Ma, 2019). With A.I. and its subsequent automation rapidly changing the nature of learning technologies, there is a pressing need for learning and development specialists to inform new developments to curate the most appropriate resources for their learning programs. Without a doubt, A.I. promises to significantly impact employees, employers, and the learning that occurs within workplaces across the globe.

While development in the A.I. space is traveling at break-neck speed, the opportunities for workplace learning have been comparatively underexplored. Whether A.I. is used to support learning analytics, automation, personalization, or adaptive learning (among many other possibilities), there are different opportunities to improve and enhance learning programs (de Laat, Joksimovic, & Ifenthaler, 2020), resulting in reduced management time, increased opportunity and improved business and learning outcomes.

Considering A.I. offers such impact and opportunity (Figure 8.2), it is worth questioning why there has been a relatively low level of uptake in workplace learning to date. This may be due to a myriad of reasons, including lack of knowledge, financial investment, and lack of skills to implement into company strategy. However, if learning professionals are overwhelmed by the offerings of A.I., as a starting point, it can be helpful for them not to focus on the intricate details of the technology itself but instead be driven by strategic learning goals that can be enhanced with simple A.I. solutions.

Personalized Learning

Personalized learning is a practice that provides tailored learning experiences to an individual. By deviating from the traditional

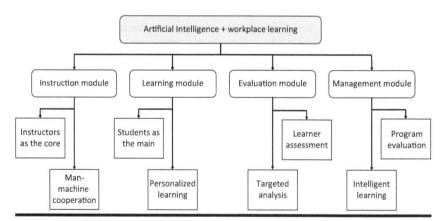

Figure 8.2 Workplace learning enhanced by artificial intelligence. Adapted from Xia (2019).

one-size-fits-all, linear approach to instruction, it recognizes the strengths and weaknesses of the learner, as well as their prior knowledge and objectives for learning, and provides educational opportunities accordingly. While a substantial body of research exists around personalized learning within school and higher education contexts, there are far fewer published studies that focus on the utilization of personalized learning within the workforce (Fake & Dabbagh, 2020).

Technology plays a crucial role in addressing learner variability and facilitating the advancement of personalized learning, and recent technological developments in this space are significant. As discussed by Lin, Zhao, Liu, and Pu (2020), the rise of A.I. and machine learning makes it possible to develop such technologies, and these are making a substantial impact in the marketplace. From smaller start-ups like Finland's Claned software, which uses a combination of A.I. and educational theories to personalize learning spaces and content (Hutchinson, 2021), to the Harvard ManageMentor Spark that can personalize business training to learners' goals and schedules (P.R. Newswire, 2019), to the explosive list of large-scale MOOCs that are emerging globally, such as FutureLearn and Degreed. With the collaborative efforts of advanced learning design, up-to-the-minute content providers, LXPs, xAPI standards, and A.I., the personalization of learning opportunities is an exciting frontier that not only holds promise but can revolutionize best practice for learning in the workplace (Figure 8.3).

However, considering the new tools and cutting-edge technologies that are making personalized learning experiences not only possible but widely dynamic and engaging (Fake & Dabbagh, 2020), the infiltration and acceptance of these experiences into company learning programs appears to be relatively slow-moving (Caboul, Chleffer, & Vaissiere, 2016), although increasing in popularity over time.

When it comes to professional development, multiple options can be maximized through differentiated pathways related to a specific worker's situation. The personal use for knowledge and skills in the workplace has become so vast and diverse, it could be said that, in general, it is no longer adequate to provide structured, undeviated learning pathways when developing in-house workplace learning programs.

Comprehensive Learner Record

The CLR, developed in association with the American Association of Collegiate Registrars and Admissions Officers (AACRAO), is an official record that specifies the learning and achievements that occur

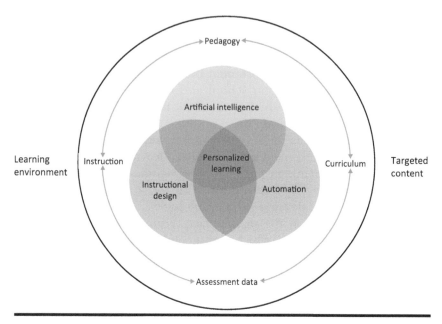

Figure 8.3   Personalized learning in the workplace.

both in and out of formal learning situations. It is a catalog of assessment data connected to the learning that is gathered from approved sources (Baker, Jankowski, & National Institute for Learning Outcomes Assessment, 2020). While the record serves as a verified profile of an individual's learning experiences over time, it is also intended to keep educational institutions transparent by clearly demonstrating the value of their offerings by connecting the learning that should occur within the courses and experiences they provide.

Every CLR has a publisher, and every achievement has an issuer, including working experiences, volunteer experiences, and formal and informal learning recognition. Achievements can come from various authorized sources and have links to competencies and skills in a range of areas. IMS Global has extended the capabilities of the CLR by certifying a list of courses and products that can be allocated to lifelong learners on secure and verifiable records. These courses can then be verified using their open-badged verification method. A learner takes ownership of their own record and can tag and track learning paths and skills and share these with others.

While the development of the CLR has served to map and document an individual's learning journey, it also creates opportunities for learning to be reimagined. It not only encourages a higher level of transparency (Baker, Jankowski, & National Institute for Learning Outcomes Assessment, 2020) from both the provider and the learner (if they choose to share their record), but it assists in the long-term mapping and progression of capabilities.

Although there is a way to go before all employers recognize the CLR as an accurate and accessible record to allow them to evaluate the capabilities of their workforce, there is potential for the technology to expand across industries and become a commonplace tool to assist in the development opportunities for education providers, employers, and individuals.

Mobile Learning

The demand for mobile and asynchronous learning is not new, but the result of the COVID-19 pandemic shifts in working and learning has seen a new wave of understanding how important this type of function actually is. Mobile learning, which can no longer be as simple as viewing desktop pages on responsive screens of varying sizes, now includes features such as augmented reality, A.I., data capture, collaboration facilities, and GPS. With a myriad of new applications flooding the marketplace (Figure 8.4), the selection of mobile learning opportunities can be somewhat overwhelming.

Growing in popularity is 'as required' mobile learning tools like WoBaLearn, (the work-based learning system) that provide

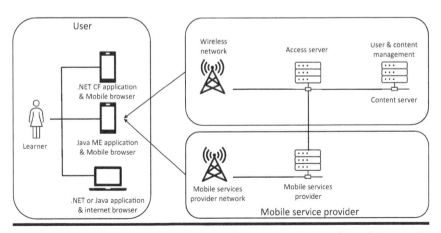

Figure 8.4   Entity architecture of an m-learning process. Adapted from Boja and Batagan (2009).

professionals with work-related support that is environment-adapted and provides learning opportunities when a person encounters difficulties. Studies by Zhang et al. (2016) report that when using WoBaLearn, workers enhance their awareness and develop their competence as the technology points to specific scenarios while providing learning support.

Ahmad and Tarmudia (2012) discuss how the perceived usefulness, self-efficacy, engagement, and adoption of mobile learning is increased in generations X, Y, and Z and suggest that due to the proportion of generation X, Y, and Z in the workplace, and the departure of much of the baby boomer generational cohort, that mobile learning opportunities are expected to be the norm as this is how learning is most commonly accessed outside of work. Regarding the 'baby boomers' and other demographics who may not share these views, Dar and Bhat (2016) carried out studies that revealed learners felt more comfortable using their own mobile devices as they were familiar with the functionality, and this reduced some of the anxiety that potentially impacted the learning outcomes.

Overall, mobile learning is an emerging and diverse technology that will clearly continue to progress. It can provide increased opportunity for personalization and potentially allows users to feel more comfortable with the technology if they are familiar with its use in other contexts.

Microlearning

Microlearning is a skill-based approach to learning that focuses on delivering small, highly focused chunks of information in a way that enables learners to find quick answers to specific questions or problems. Because people's attention spans are getting shorter and shorter all the time, we need to leverage the ability to direct interest to where it is most beneficial. Most office workers are reported to check their e-mails for up to five hours each week (Reisinger, 2018) and read very few of them in full. Similarly, as other information comes to them through a variety of sources, there is only a small percentage of the information they will actually digest.

Moreover, as the workforce becomes infiltrated with distractions and their attention spans are diminishing, individuals typically seek information via Google searches rather than through workplace training programs (Dolasinski & Reynolds, 2020). This is where microlearning can fill such information gaps without expecting the worker to invest too much time or attention into complete training packages.

Early studies on the benefits of microlearning have revealed positive outcomes, such as the study carried out by Mohammed, Wakil, & Nawroly (2018), which found that a learner's abilities increased by 18% compared to traditional methods. However, while many microlearning content providers appear, there is still little academic research to support the best practices (Dolasinski, 2020) for the implementation and ongoing management of microlearning in the workplace.

Therefore, as with any new initiative, the company must consider feedback and reviews and curate the training materials wisely. Skill mapping and other training needs analysis can be carried out at an individual level and across the entire company, leading to a valuable library of engaging learning resources available to workers.

Learning Experience Platforms

LXPs are designed to be more comprehensive, diverse, and provide a more personalized learning experience than the traditional learning management system (LMS). While there are many similarities and blurred lines between what is considered an LXP and an LMS, generally, an LMS is more static and centered around a top-down approach to instruction. At the same time, the LXP uses a bottom-up approach that is more dynamic and focused on the learner. As Betts (2020) notes, it can be difficult to source up-to-date content and curriculums for the entire business from a top-down perspective. Learning content and experiences cannot be generated fast enough to keep up with changes to business rules and technologies, and therefore he claims we should be shifting our mindset to one of ongoing self-directed learning that meets the needs and the interests of the learner. With that said, many LMSs have introduced smart searches and innovative querying features that can filter integrated content (Figure 8.5).

According to Bersin (2019), the new workplace learning paradigm has shifted from static LMS content to a need for continuous microlearning offerings. He notes a new technology stack for learning and development that includes the following elements: learning experience, skills management and assessment, curricula/career management, commerce compliance, collaboration and mentoring, course management, content management, and learning management, which is much more robust and complex than what we generally see today.

However, LXPs promise to deliver more. Within the LXP, learning experiences can be imported from various sources and managed within xAPI standards. The xAPI statement allows the capture of a variety of usage data outside of traditional learning platforms and

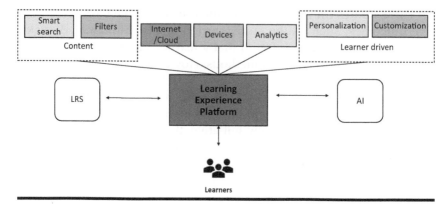

Figure 8.5   Learning Experience Platform (LXP).

stores them in the Learning Record Store (Naud & Barthelemy, 2020). Because LXPs leverage digital technologies that include a wealth of rich assets, including third-party components and content that users recommend, they can use advanced algorithms to deliver highly customized experiences. With the use of such algorithms and data analytics, LXPs can detect learning gaps and develop learning paths to bridge those gaps, often allowing the user to select their own preferences, thus, at the same time, boosting engagement.

With the promise of such targeted, up-to-date learning, personalization, and integration opportunities, there is undoubtedly a lot of potential for the LXP. At present, however, most information available on LXPs is provided by vendors, and there is very little relevant research carried out to show the real impact of LXPs in the workplace.

Conclusion

In conclusion, as digital technologies continue to shape the learning experiences in the workplace, trends are emerging that direct these experiences to be more relevant, personalized, and accessible for the individual. This chapter examined some of the influences of such trends, including changes to the composition of the workforce, the revision of the learning landscape, the rise of the digital economy, newly created workplace roles, investments in learning technologies, the need for innovation, and the decentralization of the workforce. It also looked at the technological trends themselves, which, while these are many and varied, included A.I. and automation, personalized learning experiences, CLRs, mobile learning, microlearning, and LXPs.

Overall, it is clear to see that technology is making a positive impact on learning and continues to advance at a rapid pace, enhancing the opportunities for companies to develop' their talent and improve business outcomes.

Critical Thinking Questions

1   A report by Deloitte (Schwartz, Hatfield, Jones, & Anderson, 2019) claims that the workforce, the workplace, and the work itself are all rapidly changing. What does this mean for lifelong learning?

2   Three types of skills for the digital economy have been identified by the OECD (2016) as generic skills, specialist skills, and complementary skills. How do these three skill types influence and impact one another?

3   The Comprehensive Learner Record is based on the idea of recording an individual's learning achievements across their life. This is a concept that has struggled to gain traction. Why is this so, and what are the alternatives?

4   Learning Experience Platforms are rapidly gaining popularity and increasing their capacity to deliver. Are they able to provide the learning outcomes as promised, or is further enhancement required?

5   How have the external impacts on the workplace (workforce composition, the revised learning landscape, a new suite of roles, investment in learning technologies, disruption, and decentralization) influenced the emerging technological trends for workplace learning?

References

Ahmad, M. A., & Tarmudi, S. M. (2012). Generational differences in satisfaction with e-learning among higher learning institution staff. *Procedia-Social and Behavioral Sciences, 67,* 304–311. DOI:10.1016/j. sbspro.2012.11.333

Ash, K., & Rahn, M. (2020). Reimagining workforce policy in the age of disruption: A state guide for preparing the future workforce now. *fhi360.*

Retrieved from https://www.fhi360.org/projects/future-workforce-now-reimagining-workforce-policy-age-disruption

Baker, G. R., Jankowski, N. A. (2020, June). *Documenting learning: The comprehensive learner record (Occasional Paper No. 46)*. Illinois, USA: National Institute for Learning Outcomes Assessment.

Bersin, J. (2019). *Learning technology evolves: Integrated platforms are arriving*. Josh Bersin: Insights on Corporate Talent, Learning, and H.R. Technology. Retrieved from https://joshbersin.com/2019/06/learning-technology-evolves-integrated-platforms-are-arriving/

Betts, B. (2020). Are LXPs the next best thing? *T.D. Magazine. Re*trieved from https://www.td.org/magazines/td-magazine/are-lxps-the-next-best-thing

Boja, C., & Batagan, L. (2009). Analysis of m-learning applications quality. *WSEAS Transactions on Computers archive, 8*, 767–777.

Caboul, E., Chleffer, N., & Vaissiere, C. (2016). *Adapting personal learning environments to the workplace?* Université Paris Diderot. Retrieved from https://f.hypotheses.org/wp-content/blogs.dir/1236/files/2016/10/Article_AdaptingPLE.pdf.

Chen, J., Yin, X., & Mei, L. (2018). Holistic innovation: an emerging innovation paradigm. *International Journal of Innovation Studies, 2*(1), 1–13.

Dan Andrei, M. (2019). Innovation and Competitiveness. *Annals of the University of Oradea, Economic Science Series, 28*(2), 385–394.

Dar, M. A., & Bhat, S. A. (2016, September). *Evaluation of mobile learning in workplace training*. In *2016 International Conference on Advances in Computing, Communications and Informatics (ICACCI)* (pp. 1468–1473). IEEE. DOI:10.1109/ICACCI.2016.7732255

Dean, B. A., & Campbell, M. (2020). Reshaping work-integrated learning in a post-COVID-19 world of work. *International Journal of Work-Integrated Learning, 21*(4), 355–364.

Delaney, R., & D'Agostino, R. (2015). *The challenges of integrating new technology into an organization*. [Doctoral dissertation, LaSalle University]. LaSalle Digital Commons Mathematics and Computer Science Capstones, 25. Retrieved from https://digitalcommons.lasalle.edu/mathcompcapstones/25

De Laat, M., Joksimovic, S., & Ifenthaler, D. (2020). Artificial intelligence, real-time feedback and workplace learning analytics to support in situ complex problem-solving: A commentary. *International Journal of Information and Learning Technology, 37*(5), 267–277. DOI:10.1108/IJILT-03-2020-0026

Dolasinski, M. J., & Reynolds, J. (2020). Microlearning: a new learning model. *Journal of Hospitality & Tourism Research, 44*(3), 551–561. DOI:10.1177/1096348002091579

Fake, H., & Dabbagh, N. (2020). Personalized learning within online work-force learning environments: Exploring implementations, obstacles, opportunities, and perspectives of workforce leaders. *Technology, Knowledge and Learning, 25*, 1–21. DOI:10.1007/s10758-020-09441-x

Gray, A. (2017). *The four levels of computer skills, and the surprising number of adults who fail*. Retrieved from https://www.weforum.org/agenda/2017/02/a-quarter-of-adults-can-t-use-a-computer/

Hutchinson, C. (2021). The claned online learning model. *Claned*. Retrieved April 15, 2021 from https://claned.com/the-claned-online-learning-model/

Lin, J., Zhao, Y., Liu, C., & Pu, H. (2020, June). *Personalized learning service based on big data for education*. In *2020 IEEE 2nd International Conference on Computer Science and Educational Informatization (CSEI)* (pp. 235–238). Xinxiang, China: IEEE.

Markets and Markets. (2020). *Learning management system market global forecast to 2025. By component (solution and services), delivery mode (distance learning, instructor-led training, and blended learning), deployment type, user type (academic and corporate), and region*. Markets and Markets. Retrieved from https://www.marketsandmarkets.com/Market-Reports/learning-management-systems-market-1266.html

Merriam-Webster. (2021). Trend. *Merriam-Webster.com dictionary*. Retrieved from https://www.merriam-webster.com/dictionary/trends

Mohammed, G. S., Wakil, K., & Nawroly, S. S. (2018). The effectiveness of microlearning to improve student's learning ability. *International Journal of Educational Research Review, 3*(3), 32–38. DOI: 10.24331/ijere.415824

Nakata, C. (2020). Design thinking for innovation: Considering distinctions, fit, and use in firms. *Business Horizons, 63*(6), 763–772. DOI: 10.1016/j.bushor.2020.07.008

Naud, M., & Barthelemy, M. (2020). *The great guide to learning experience platforms*. Blink. Retrieved from https://bealink.io/en/learning-experience-platform-great-guide/

Nielsen, C., Dotiwala, F., & Murray, M. (2020). *A transformation of the learning function: Why it should learn new ways*. McKinsey and Company. Retrieved from https://www.mckinsey.com/business-functions/mckinsey-accelerate/our-insights/a-transformation-of-the-learning-function-why-it-should-learn-new-ways

Organisation for Economic Co-operation and Development. (2016). *Technical Report of the Survey of Adult Skills (PIAAC)*. Retrieved from Retrieved from http://www.oecd.org/skills/piaac/publications.html

Reisinger, D. (2018). *You spend more than 5 hours each week checking your e-mail*. Fortune.com. Retrieved from https://fortune.com/2018/08/21/email-habits-attention-study-adobe/

P.R. Newswire. (2019, March 14). Harvard business publishing corporate learning and degreed partner on a learning experience that reflects the needs of today's learners. *P.R. Newswire U.S.*

Russell, S. J., & Norvig, P. (2014). *Artificial intelligence: A modern approach* (3rd ed.). London: Pearson.

Schwartz, J., Hatfield, R., Jones, R., & Anderson, S. (2019). *What is the future of work? Redefining work, workforces, and workplaces.* Deloitte Insights. Retrieved from https://www2.deloitte.com/us/en/insights/focus/technology-and-the-future-of-work/redefining-work-workforces-workplaces.html

Shimkus, D. (2019). *Learning is worth the investment, and the numbers back it up.* Forbes. Retrieved from https://www.forbes.com/sites/darrenshimkus/2019/04/10/learning-is-worth-the-investment-the-numbers-back-it-up

Spector, J., & Ma, S. (2019). Inquiry and critical thinking skills for the next generation: From artificial intelligence back to human intelligence. *Smart Learning Environments, 6*(1), 1–11, DOI:10.1186/s40561-019-0088-z

Spiezia, V., Koksal-Oudot, E., & Montagnier, P. (2016). *New skills for the digital economy measuring the demand and supply of ICT skills at work.* OECD iLibrary. DOI:10.1787/5jlwnkm2fc9x-en

Totterdill, P. (2013, December 5). *Workplace innovation: the fifth element [Video] YouTube.* Retrieved from https://www.youtube.com/watch?v=hutLABOniCc

U.S. Bureau of Labor Statistics. (2019). *Number of jobs, labor market experience, and earnings growth: Results from a national longitudinal survey.* BLS. Retrieved from https://www.bls.gov/news.release/pdf/nlsoy.pdf

Verhoef, P. C., Broekhuizen, T., Bart, Y., Bhattacharya, A., Dong, J. Q., Fabian, N., & Haenlein, M. (2019). Digital transformation: A multidisciplinary reflection and research agenda. *Journal of Business Research, 122,* 889–901. DOI:10.1016/j.jbusres.2019.09.022

Wilson, S. (2013). *Thinking differently about leadership: A critical history of leadership studies.* Cheltenham, UK: Edward Elgar Publishing.

Xia, P. (2019). *Application scenario of artificial intelligence technology in higher education.* In *International Conference on Applications and Techniques in Cyber Security and Intelligence* (pp. 221–226). Cham: Springer.

Zhang, B., Yin, C., David, B., Xiong, Z., & Niu, W. (2016). Facilitating professionals' work-based learning with context-aware mobile system. *Science of Computer Programming, 129,* 3–19. DOI:10.1016/j.scico.2016.01.008

Chapter 9

EdTech for the Modern Start-up

While this book primarily focuses on learning in the workplace, for the purposes of discussing start-up potential in the education space, we examine the broader field of education including early learning, school education, higher education, workplace learning, and lifelong learning opportunities. Improving the educational landscape across this spectrum ultimately leads to improved workplace learning attitudes, scenarios, and directions for the next generation.

It is often said that historical times of crisis, such as the global COVID-19 pandemic, are the accelerators and drivers of significant innovation and change (Hershock, 2020). Amidst ongoing educational reform around the world, it is clear that the future of education and training hinges on technological advancements in many ways. From artificial intelligence to virtual reality, big data to adaptive learning, educational technologies rapidly change and reveal opportunities for further development.

This chapter examines the educational technology (EdTech) that is enabling educators and organizations to improve performance and increase the potential of individuals. We consider the opportunities for modern start-ups in this field and the marketplace for such technologies. Then, we examine barriers to entry, the types of technologies required, and the problems that may need to be solved. We go on to discuss the entrepreneurial spirit and its suitability for the industry before finally considering common points of failure and the opportunities provided by incubators. This chapter is important to include as the digital age is revolutionizing the ways people learn, and when backed by a thriving entrepreneurial energy, opportunities can be tapped into that we previously thought of as inconceivable.

A Promising Marketplace

There is an ongoing digital transformation occurring that encompasses all elements of business and government activities (Mattsson & Andersson, 2019). This transformation dramatically affects the education industry and educational reform worldwide, as nations prioritize the preparation of their workforces for the future and realize that technology can enable education, training, and lifelong learning, leading to improved outcomes for all (Ash & Rahn, 2020).

This transformation was sharply accelerated when the COVID-19 pandemic forced significant regions of the world to embrace online learning practically overnight. Despite the dilemmas that were faced, it became clear that EdTech not only makes things possible but serves as a huge opportunity to improve the entire industry. Hershock (2020) points out that crises can serve as drivers of opportunity and that the COVID-19 pandemic is the first truly global health crisis of the smartphone era.

Educational technology originally served a straightforward function: to provide learners with access to electronic educational materials. However, the growing demand for educational solutions has prompted businesses, universities, schools, and colleges to invest in many high-tech solutions. EdTech now includes everything from the online classroom to cutting-edge developments in artificial intelligence, immersive technologies such as virtual and augmented reality, adaptive learning, and gamification (Hershock, 2020).

Start-up hubs all over the world are bringing proven ideas into the marketplace. Working with education departments to discover their requirements and build solutions for them drives overall growth, and governments, private actors, and investors are taking notice. The appetite for EdTech is undoubtedly there, and as early as 2018, the EdTech market was predicted to increase from a global $157 billion to $420 billion by 2025 (Hershock, 2020), and this was *before* the global shift to online learning. These figures are predicted to rise significantly further over the coming decade as the need for online education has soared.

In addition to this, investors are demonstrating a strong interest in EdTech, as seen in the year 2020, which brought a record-breaking investment to the sector, raising over $10.76 billion across the world within 12 months. The magnitude of this investment is apparent when compared to the $4.7 billion raised in 2019 (Tech Crunch, 2021). In the United States alone, venture capital injected $1.78 billion across 265 EdTech start-up projects in 2020 compared to $1.32 billion in 2019 (Tech Crunch, 2021). Increasingly, it also seems that investors are attracted to start-ups that are targeting real educational issues and offering significant value to students, which ties in with societal values and corporate responsibility.

Reduced Barriers to Entry

Several significant breakthroughs have made the delivery of EdTech solutions more possible than ever before. Obvious developments with widespread internet connectivity and Wi-Fi, access to the cloud, and the repository of open-source projects enhance the potential to design, develop and deliver. Coupled with the ability to tap into resources online and outsource much of the development, this reduces some of the previous barriers to entry in the EdTech space (Figure 9.1).

Hershock (2020) claims there is an unprecedented opportunity for scaling rapidly from proof-of-concept to the mass implementation of

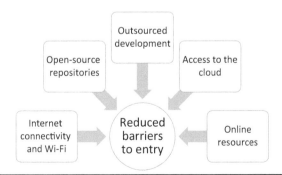

Figure 9.1   Reduced barriers to entry for educational technology start-ups.

cutting-edge educational technologies due to the global pandemic. Investors and incubators are increasing globally, and start-ups with true solutions can find promising opportunities. It is worth noting, however, that cutting-edge solutions are required for big educational problems. There has been a strong focus on lean methodologies that focus on minimum viable products (MVPs) in the mainstream start-up vicinity. Felin, Gambardella, Stern, and Zenger (2019) explain that the lean start-up embraces the idea of developing and testing products and ideas quickly and reiterating the design once stakeholder feedback is provided. However, they also go on to suggest that some of the most valuable ideas for education are actually ones that cannot be rapidly designed and tested and need much deeper consideration. Suppose entrepreneurs genuinely want to deliver ideas that will 'disrupt' an industry. In that case, they may need more time spent in the research phase, considering the real problems and potential solutions rather than merely looking for the low-hanging fruit that can be designed, tested, and developed quickly.

Therefore, when considering that the lean start-up approach may have been designed for manufacturing products that lead to incremental but relatively safe innovation, alternative methods may be required for the true entrepreneur who wishes to deliver something radically new (Felin et al., 2019). Perhaps the answer lies in breaking down the components of a more extensive solution and running several MVPs in parallel sprints (Figure 9.2), allowing ideas to be tested and refined while reaching for more complex solutions. However, while there may be reduced barriers to entry, there are still many obstacles and risks worth serious consideration, such as product differentiation, capital requirements, access to distribution channels, legal requirements, and government policies.

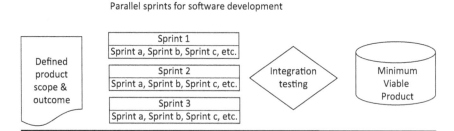

Figure 9.2   Parallel sprints for developing more complex EdTech solutions.

The interwoven digitization and innovation processes sought by EdTech start-ups can sometimes clash with public sectors like education in the ways they operate (Mattsson & Andersson, 2019). Government service models are complex, and private actors need to pre-empt these obstructions and adapt their business models and expectations to allow for the tensions that may be experienced throughout their transactions (Mattsson & Andersson, 2019). (Figure 9.3).

Influencing policy decisions regarding education may be something worth putting on the agenda. Although many government departments claim inclusivity when developing policies, and the OECD (2014) recommends that digital government strategies concerned with the transformation of public services (i.e., enhancing educational services through the use of EdTech) should engage stakeholders of public, private, and civil society to collaborate on making policies around design and delivery, these things may not always occur in reality. In addition to this, even when a national policy supports an EdTech solution, national school, procurement, and digitization policies trickle down to the local levels in various ways through a complex network of public organizations (Mattsson & Andersson, 2019). This can result in a disjointed mismatch of suitable solutions and worthwhile investment. (I.e., a local school may realize

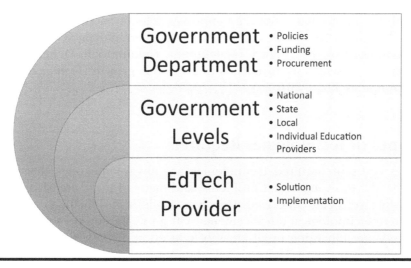

Figure 9.3 Complexities involved with implementing technology into government departments.

the EdTech solution is suitable for their problem, but an overarching digitization or procurement policy from their state may deter them from investing).

The Entrepreneurial Spirit

Entrepreneurs are forward thinkers who cultivate new ideas and inspire those around them. They encourage innovation to solve problems, discover new opportunities and solutions, and breathe the necessary vitality into long-term organizational growth. The entrepreneurial spirit is a mindset, attitude, and approach that is usually leveraged by an innate kind of enthusiasm. While many entrepreneurial courses can be taken, some might say it is not something that can be easily learned and is more of a character trait that certain individuals possess. However, if taught from an early age and inspired by the possibilities of their future, it could be a tacit skill that is transferred. Entrepreneurs see problems as opportunities, challenges as tasks to be overcome, and change as a constant state of being.

Entrepreneurial competencies are gaining interest throughout society as more people are becoming aware of their qualities. These competencies are actively being taught in many academic courses in countries such as the United States, Canada, India, and South Korea, with the intent that it not only improves self-confidence and creativity but that these skills contribute to fuller employment and more innovation for the country (Malekipour, Hakimzadeh, Dehghani, & Zali, 2017), which in turn, leads to economic growth (Mehta, Zappe, Brannon, & Zhao, 2016).

Types of Technologies Required

The types of required technologies are always the ones that will solve the most important problems, and many of these are ideas that haven't yet been conceived. However, while it is difficult to predict where technological advancements will go in the future, some clear trends are emerging in all areas of education, from early childhood to lifelong learning. These include, but are in no way limited to, solutions based on mobile applications, immersive technologies, learning analytics, artificial intelligence, and gamification.

Mobile Applications

Mobile applications for education often referred to as m-learning, are surging in popularity. Because mobile devices offer one of the quickest and easiest ways to access educational content, they can reduce the barriers to entry. However, this also contributes to making m-learning a very crowded marketplace. The benefits of m-learning include its ability to encourage and anytime-anywhere learning habit, and it can also contribute to closing the so-called learning divide (Drigas & Angelidakis, 2017). However, there are educational draw-backs that include a potential lack of socialization, issues with connectivity and updates, and challenges with support.

Mobile learning applications are arguably more popular among younger people as they tend to be more fluent with the technology. However, workplace learning applications have more room to be explored. Mobile devices offer one of the easiest and fastest ways to access educational content. Besides World Wide Web, mobile devices have their own set-up application store where users can download unique apps. All these apps are designed with a specific purpose. Consider gaming apps that have an entertaining purpose. Still, the possibilities are endless, and many games are developed with an edu-cational orientation.

Immersive Technologies

Immersive technologies include virtual, augmented, and blended real-ity experiences, and these experiences tend to be deeper and more contextual due to the emphasis on the full process of an individual's involvement in what is being learned (Ekstrand et al., 2018; Surya & Putri, 2017). While immersive technologies, particularly virtual real-ity, are relatively expensive to develop, the field shows a longer-term progression that is promising to disrupt the education industry.

Virtual reality can also incur a very costly initial setup for the end users, making it more limited in appeal to many government-funded institutions. Whereas augmented reality overlays can be used on the user's mobile device, making them a cheaper and easier alternative. However, all immersive technologies have a place in education, as stud-ies reveal there are clear benefits for using virtual and augmented real-ities for learning in many industries, including medicine, military, and higher education (Ahir, Govani, Gajera, & Shah, 2020; Awoke et al., 2021;

Rogers, DeSantis, Janjua, Barry, & Kuo, 2020), and it is an area that will be very interesting to watch as the field develops further.

Learning Analytics

There is potential for learning analytics to bring about improved educational outcomes as it identifies the strengths and weaknesses of training programs. Learning analytics draw on data sets that provide real-time insights to enhance learning (Ifenthaler, 2020).

As with data analytics in general, there is a huge increase in attention to these tools as they essentially record and report the results and trends that can inform improved practice. Because data comes from various sources and is mined for a variety of reasons, there is a requirement for standards to be utilized to bring these sources together (Williamson, 2014). Standards such as the Experience (x) API or the IMS Global Caliper Framework can bring this information together into one central repository.

Artificial Intelligence

Artificial intelligence (A.I.) and the automation of repetitive activity are rising dramatically in both popularity and complexity. A.I. can enable personalized and adaptive learning and streamline the creation, assessment, and program evaluation, among many other things. A popular example of personalized and adaptive learning informed by A.I. are popular artificial tutor systems used in China and other countries, such as *Squirrel*. The system breaks down content into the smallest manageable chunks and sequences them so that students can learn what they need, and skip what they don't need, to fill the gaps in their knowledge (Hao, 2020).

The vision for A.I. in education is one where automation and instructors can work together to complement the attributes of the other. Since the future of work will also feature A.I. in a significant way, it is an educational tool that assists students with learning while exposing and familiarizing them to the technology at the same time.

Gamification

Gamification is described as applying game design elements in a non-game, learning context (Zichermann & Cunningham, 2011), often including such elements as points, levels, goals, and status. As research shows that educational games used for learning increase problem-solving and collaboration skills (Drigas & Angelidakis, 2017) and self-efficacy and productivity (Ofosu-Ampong, 2020), it is not surprising that gamification for education is a rapidly growing marketplace. The engaging nature of game-style learning enables more students to access, participate, and achieve learning outcomes.

While very popular in the classroom, gamification is often overlooked for workplace training (Figure 9.4). There is potential to expand this field and incorporate it with A.I. and immersive technologies for truly targeted workplace learning experiences. However, regardless of the target audience, studies carried out by Ofosu-Ampong (2020) reveal the importance of understanding the nature of the educational institution and the end users before designing a game because failing to do so often leads to gamification failure.

As stated above, there are many types of technologies that can solve user problems, and these are only scraping the surface of what is possible. While the opportunities could be considered potentially limitless, Tech Crunch (2021) recommends steering away from developing copycat technologies like standard online learning platforms and moving toward new takes on more advanced technologies such as artificial intelligence solutions, neurolinguistic programming, machine learning, and virtual reality-style applications. What is ultimately important, however, is that EdTech solves the big education problems.

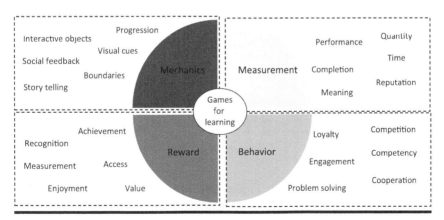

Figure 9.4 Gamification model. Adapted from Wahid (2018).

Identifying Problems

There are an infinite number of problems within the field of education and training throughout the world. These problems can range from extreme issues, like safe access to school in some developing countries, to simple issues such as increasing the speed that a teacher can mark their students' work. Regardless of where the problem sits on the spectrum, however, it needs to be a real problem for the end user in mind.

As the basis of a start-up, it's important to seek the best possible problems to solve. The best problem is the one that resonates with its potential users and sits at the heart of what they are trying to accomplish. The issue should be so pressing for the user that they are willing to take the extra steps to learn about and invest in the solution and subsequently learn how to implement and utilize the resulting EdTech product (Figure 9.5).

Here are some widespread problems that may benefit significantly from the acquisition of the right EdTech solutions. (The solutions are not provided in this book, as the problems are merely presented as examples to ignite the entrepreneur's creativity).

Online Learning Challenges

While online learning may have been increasing in popularity over time, its widespread adoption was practically forced on millions due

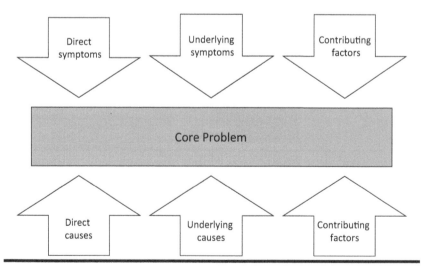

Figure 9.5 Defining core problems.

to the COVID-19 pandemic. Because of the speed of this change, there were many difficulties to adaptation. Still, since online learning has been adopted so widely, more educators see the opportunity and value of online learning.

Malkawi and Khayrullina (2021) carried out studies on 2347 university students who participated in online learning and revealed three groups of problems they encountered, which were (1) obtaining feedback from tutors, (2) concentration and self-management, and (3) technical difficulties associated with staying connected. The market for online learning is expanding and deepening, as a variety of content, applications, formats, and platforms are enabling improved and interconnected opportunities.

Generalized Learning

One-size-fits-all learning is something that millions are familiar with across the world. Traditionally, educational curriculums have been developed with one learning path in mind and sequenced so that each individual progresses through the content at the same time, regardless of their previous experience or the context in which they are acquiring the new knowledge.

In contrast to generalized learning is personalized learning, which refers to content and experiences that are designed and paced to meet the needs of each individual learner. To take this one step further, adaptive learning focuses on the use of personal data and technologies that automatically evaluate and update the content as learning unfolds (Peng, Ma, & Spector, 2019).

While there have been efforts made in recent times to improve generalized learning, there is still plenty of room for advancement. Personalization and adaptive learning are enhanced by artificial intelligence and learning analytics, along with the creative integration of other technologies, and there are global markets that are eager to invest in these technologies.

Student Engagement and Participation

A significant issue in education from early childhood through to workplace training is the difficulty with engaging the learner and encouraging their active participation. Particularly when learning online, when many learners are displaced or remote, relying on their instructor to spoon-feed them is no longer feasible. Technological advancements can bypass the need for such reliance on individual instructors and free them to work on targeted support.

Applying game mechanics and other interactive and entertaining dynamics to learning can increase user engagement (Muntean, 2011) and assist with knowledge construction. Noting that most people, particularly young people, choose to be engaging with their electronic devices as often as possible, there are opportunities to emulate these engaging activities in an educational context. Consider virtual reality producers such as Bohemia Interactive, who develop programs to enable military training. The popularity of these engaging technologies is so widespread that their spin-off military games are best sellers (Bohemia interactive, 2017).

Quality Education across the Globe

The biggest problems of all are those outlined within The United Nations Targets' fourth goal: Quality Education (The United Nations, 2019). These areas would benefit from advancements in EdTech that could perhaps provide solutions that hadn't been considered before. The potential that many young entrepreneurs have to invent entirely new ways of bringing a solution to life is there, and by focusing on these real-world issues, the benefits reaped would be too great for words. Solving these problems can literally change the future for millions of people across the globe. Some of the problems outlined and waiting to be solved are:

1. The completion of primary and secondary school for all children.

This is an issue for many families who require their children to work or don't understand why their girls should be educated. Solutions here may include providing digital learning opportunities from the home or education to families and communities about the importance of education.

2. Access to quality early childhood development.

This could potentially be improved by providing accessible learning technologies to pre-primary-aged children, training trainers, and educating parents.

3. Affordable and quality technical vocational and tertiary education.

EdTech solutions that support government and corporate partner-ships to repurpose and share quality resources may contribute to solving this problem.

4. Substantially increase the number of youth and adults who have the relevant skills required for decent jobs.

The provision of widespread, affordable learning resources and the knowledge of how to learn and why to learn may assist with this problem, which by many accounts is predicted to get far worse in the coming decades (Harari, 2019; Kelly, 2017).

5. Equal access to education for women, people with disabilities, indigenous people, and those otherwise disadvantaged.

EdTech is producing some incredible solutions for all types of people with disadvantages, and these areas can continue to expand creatively.

6. All youth and a substantial proportion of adults should achieve literacy and numeracy.

Again, widespread, affordable access to reusable resources may con-tribute to alleviating this issue and improving the lives of millions. Also, for many, this is the key to obtaining further education in any of the areas mentioned above or below.

7. All learners should acquire the skills and knowledge needed to promote sustainable development.

EdTech solutions might incorporate devices that last for more years, being updated rather than replaced, as this saves the cost to the envi-ronment on device production (Ash-Brown, Priest, Kioupi, & O'Reilly, 2021). They may also engage learners using creative mediums to pro-mote human rights, gender equality, peace, global citizenship, and appreciation of cultural diversity.

8. Substantially increase the supply of qualified teachers.

The EdTech solutions here may be limitless. Partnering with govern-ments to roll out accessible, up-to-date, and concise digital education to teachers will be highly beneficial for all stakeholders, particularly the students.

Problem Statements

Once a problem has been defined, it is helpful to write out a problem statement including a description of who has the problem and why it is a problem for them (Figure 9.6). This assists in working toward the solutions.

The next step in the exploratory process can be to seek the opportunities that already exist. In the field of education, there are always governments, NGOs, and private bodies who are investing money to solve particular problems. It is at these times when the organizations have already committed to making investments and seeking solutions that the new ideas may be more likely to be considered. One such example is the government of the Indian state of Kerala committed to transforming their economy by fostering an innovative society throughout their state. As part of this objective, they sought opportunities to bring more innovation to their students. As a result, they engaged the Massachusetts Institute of Technology Fab Labs into 150

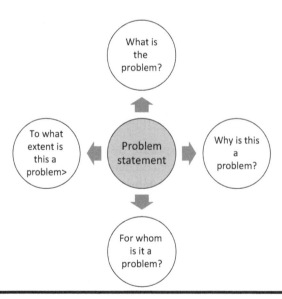

Figure 9.6 Formulating a problem statement.

of their technical schools to aid with this transformation (Ash & Rahn, 2020). This illustrates that when keeping up-to-date with educational targets and investments, opportunities for partnership may be more likely to become apparent.

EdTech Incubators

Although the entrepreneurial spirit is alive and well, and many educational problems throughout the world may benefit from creative EdTech solutions, there are also limits to what can be achieved. With the start-up's focus likely to be on big ideas and time to market, there are often gaps in experience with creating and running a company.

EdTech incubators, which are typically sponsored programs that aim to launch EdTech start-ups are an ideal solution to test ideas and business models. While general technology incubators have been increasing in popularity over time, there has more recently been an expanding number of specialized EdTech models emerging. Companies such as Imagine K12 merged with Y Combinator in 2016 and were among the first serious EdTech accelerators that were explicitly designed to enable entrepreneurs to navigate the unique intricacies of education (Australian Trade and Investment Commission, 2017).

Many EdTech incubators have been modeled after Silicon Valley's Y Combinator (which launched huge start-ups like Airbnb and Zenefits) and are experiencing significant success. Incubators such as Imagine K12, SIIA Innovation Incubator Program, 4.0 Schools, StartI, Socratic Labs, and MacMillan New Ventures have enabled serious EdTech start-ups with increasing success. When entrepreneurs are focused on developing an idea and bringing it to market, and they are mentored through an EdTech incubator, they can consequently concentrate on their product, while mentors assist them with complexities such as; legal issues, government policies, cybersecurity, funding, identity management, API standards, and networking opportunities.

Conclusion

As ongoing educational reform, the digital revolution and the global pandemic have accelerated innovation and change, the education marketplace is seeking new solutions to new problems. As the appetite for investment in EdTech is at an all-time high, and the barriers to entry are at an all-time low, there is an opportunity for entrepreneurs to discover creative solutions that can solve problems around the world and improve learning outcomes for all.

Through the further development of technologies such as mobile applications, immersive technologies, artificial intelligence, learning analytics, and gamification, digital technologies can reach more people and solve more problems worldwide. By nurturing the entrepreneurial spirit and leveraging EdTech incubators, there are many start-up ideas that have the potential to excel now and into the future.

According to Pierce and Cleary (2016), the United States is in a good position to implement educational technologies comprehensively across all states. The societal returns would potentially be very significant. In addition to this, the economic benefits to the country over the longer term will also accrue as the next generation can master the knowledge and skills necessary for the workplaces of the future.

EdTech is revolutionizing the ways people learn, and when backed by innovative entrepreneurial communities, there are opportunities to tap into real problems and make a difference to the future of education.

Critical Thinking Questions

1   In what ways has technology revolutionized the ways in which education can be experienced and delivered?
2   What entrepreneurial qualities can lead to improved social outcomes and how does education feed into this?
3   For educational technologies to have the greatest impact on improving learning outcomes, why should standards such as xAPI be considered?
4   Humanitarian issues such as access to education and gender inequality are unlikely to be resolved with the use of mobile applications. Instead, how can a bigger, more scalable solution be realized through the use of digital technologies?
5   Technology needn't be a standalone concept and can instead be used to drive other initiatives. Using technology as a driver, how can environmental issues be impacted through education?

References

Ahir, K., Govani, K., Gajera, R., & Shah, M. (2020). Application on virtual reality for enhanced education learning, military training, and sports. *Augmented Human Research*, *5*, 7. DOI:10.1007/s41133-019-0025-2

Ash, K., & Rahn, M. (2020). Reimagining workforce policy in the age of disruption: A state guide for preparing the future workforce now. *National Governors Association*.

Ash-Brown, G., Priest, C., Kioupi, V. & O'Reilly, K. (2021, April 14). How can edtech help steer us towards sustainability goals? [Video file]. Retrieved from https://edtechnology.co.uk/roundtables/how-can-edtech-help-steer-us-towards-sustainability-goals/

Australian Trade and Investment Commission. (2017). *EdTech US market snapshot*. Australian Government. Retrieved February 2, 2021, from https://www.austrade.gov.au/australian/education/news/reports/edtech-us-market-snapshot

Awoke, A., Burbelo, H., Childs, E., Mohammad, F., Stevens, L., Rewkowski, N., & Manocha, D. (2021). *An overview of enhancing distance learning through augmented and virtual reality technologies*. Cornell University. Retrieved from https://arxiv.org/abs/2101.11000

Bohemia Interactive Simulations Launches Augmented Reality Visual System for TRU Simulation + Training. (2017, November 30). *Entertainment Close-Up*. Retrieved from https://search.ebscohost.com/login.aspx?direct=true&AuthType=sso&db=edsggo&AN=edsgcl.516429998&site=eds-live&scope=site

Drigas, A. S., & Angelidakis, P. (2017). Mobile applications within education: An overview of application paradigms in specific categories. *International Journal of Interactive Mobile Technologies*, *11*(4), 17–29. DOI:10.3391/ijim.v11i4.6589

Ekstrand, C., Jamal, A., Nguyen, R., Kudryk, A., Mann, J., & Mendez, I. (2018). Immersive and interactive virtual reality to improve learning and retention of neuroanatomy in medical students: A randomized controlled study. *CMAJ Open*, *6*(1), 103–109. DOI:10.9778/cmajo.20170110

Felin, T., Gambardella, A., Stern, S., & Zenger, T. (2019). Lean start-up and the business model: Experimentation revisited. *Forthcoming in Long Range Planning (Open Access)*. Retrieved from https://ssrn.com/abstract=3427084

Hao, K. (2020). Born in China, taught by A.I. *MIT Technology Review*, *123*(1), 24–29. Retrieved from https://eds.a.ebscohost.com/eds/pdfviewer/pdfviewer?vid=3&sid=1d4b2192-5632-4ad8-9209-35e26a474859%40sdc-v-sessmgr03

Harari, Y. (2019). *21 lessons for the 21st Century*. London: Random House.

Hershock, P. (2020). *Humane artificial intelligence: Inequality, social cohesion and the post-pandemic acceleration of intelligent technology.* East-West Center. DOI:10.2307/resrep25513

Ifenthaler, D. (2020). Change management for learning analytics. In N. Pinkwart & S. Liu (Eds.), *Artificial intelligence supported educational technologies* (pp. 261–272). Springer. DOI:10.1007/978-3-030-41099-5_15

Kelly, K. (2017). *The inevitable – understanding the 12 technological forces that will shape our future.* New York: Penguin Group.

Malekipour, A., Hakimzadeh, R., Dehghani, M., & Zali, M. R. (2017). Content analysis of curriculum syllabus for the educational technology discipline based on entrepreneurial competencies. *Interdisciplinary Journal of Virtual Learning in Medical Sciences, 8*(4), e62156. DOI:10.5812/ijvlms.62156

Malkawi, E., & Khayrullina, M. (2021). Digital learning environment in higher education: New global issues. *SHS Web of Conferences, 92*(3), 05019. DOI:10.1051/shsconf/20219205019

Mattsson, L. G., & Andersson, P. (2019). Private-public interaction in public service innovation processes-business model challenges for a start-up EdTech firm. *Journal of Business & Industrial Marketing, 34*(5), 1106–1118. DOI:10.1108/JBIM-10-2018-0297

Mehta, K., Zappe, S., Brannon, M. L., & Zhao, Y. (2016). An educational and entrepreneurial ecosystem to actualize technology-based social ventures. *Advances in Engineering Education, 5*(1), 1–38.

Muntean, C. I. (2011, October). Raising engagement in e-learning through gamification. In *Proceedings of the 6th International Conference on Virtual Learning* (Vol. *1*, pp. 323–329). Romania: ICVL..

OECD (2014). *Innovating the public sector: From ideas to impact. OECD Conference Proceedings.*

Ofosu-Ampong, K. (2020). The shift to gamification in education: A review on dominant issues. *Journal of Educational Technology Systems, 49*(1), 113–137. DOI:10.1177/0047239520917629

Peng, H., Ma, S., & Spector, J. M. (2019). Personalized adaptive learning: An emerging pedagogical approach enabled by a smart learning environment. *Smart Learning Environments, 6*(1), 9. DOI:10.1186/s40561-019-0089-y

Pierce, G. L., & Cleary, P. F. (2016). The K-12 educational technology value chain: Apps for kids, tools for teachers and levers for reform. *Education and Information Technologies, 21*(4), 863–880. DOI:10.1007/s10639-014-9357-1

Tech Crunch. (2021). *13 ways investors say lifelong learning is taking edtech mainstream.* Retrieved from https://techcrunch.com/2021/01/28/12-investors-say-lifelong-learning-is-taking-edtech-mainstream/

The United Nations. (2019). *Sustainable development goals*. United Nations. Retrieved September 28, 2020, from https://www.un.org/sustainabledevelopment/education/

Rogers, M. P., DeSantis, A. J., Janjua, H., Barry, T. M., & Kuo, P. C. (2020). The future surgical training paradigm: Virtual reality and machine learning in surgical education. *Surgery*. Advance online publication. DOI:10.1016/j.surg.2020.09.040

Surya, E., & Putri, F. A. (2017). Improving mathematical problem-solving ability and self-confidence of high school students through contextual learning model. *Journal on Mathematics Education*, 8(1), 85–94. DOI:10.22342/jme.8.1.3324.85-94

Wahid, S. (2018). *The effectiveness of gamification in improving student performance for programming lesson*. Research Gate.

Williamson, J. (2014). *An overview of learning analytics*. UCLA Office of Information Technology. www.wikihub.berkeley.edu.

Zichermann, G., & Cunningham, C. (2011). *Gamification by design: Implementing game mechanics in web and mobile apps*. Massachusetts, USA: O'Reilly Media.

Conclusion

Technology-enhanced learning is changing the way we perceive and access ongoing development opportunities in the workplace. As we grapple with understanding how the workplace will look in the decades to come, what we know for sure is that it will be shaped by technology. Businesses and individuals alike are putting ongoing learning at the forefront of future development, and this adoption will only strengthen. As we now understand, skillsets and knowledge are everchanging, meaning that continuous adaptation and revision is the only way to maintain peak performance.

This book examined the digital technologies that are emerging in the workplace and can support online learning. While the list of topics was by no means exhaustive, we examined emerging trends and considered them through the lens of lifelong learning. The first section of the book conveyed the current impacts on the workplace and discussed how the internal learning and development function has evolved. It also considered eight learning imperatives that underpin successful online learning before exploring three predicted future scenarios. In the middle section of the book, we looked at three technological frameworks that may enhance long-term, sustainable workplace learning. It then took a closer look at how learning analytics can inform quality learning programs and the expanding potential of immersive technologies for education. The final section gave insight into the emerging digital learning trends, as well as consideration for modern EdTech start-ups that might solve real-world educational problems across the globe.

It is with great hope that business leaders, learning and development professionals, and individuals alike will embrace lifelong learning and prioritize workplace learning in the future. The alignment of

DOI: 10.1201/9781003149132-11

lifelong learning to continuous growth is clear, particularly for individuals and their personal outcomes in and outside the workplace. As the world continues to evolve and technology hastens the speed of change, this is a ride we can choose to take and harness, rather than being overridden by technological advancements as passive bystanders. Workplace learning will never be the same as it was a decade ago. It has changed enormously and will continue to expand as the way we work and operate becomes a direct result of our interactions with technologies and the skills and knowledge we've learned.

While each chapter in this book focuses on a different topic, they are all aimed to inform and inspire lifelong learning and the way we view ongoing training in the workplace. There were critical thinking questions offered at the end of each chapter with the goal to inspire the reader to think more openly about how we can improve educational outcomes with the use of digital technology. Hopefully, the coming years will see organizations investing more in the ongoing learning of their workforce and raising the profile of continuous education. It is also hoped that individuals will seek to define their own learning plans for the future and think creatively about how their professional pathways can be supported by such education. As, relevant to both businesses and individuals are the words of Albert Einstein, "once you stop learning, you start dying."

Index

Page numbers in *italic* indicate figures.

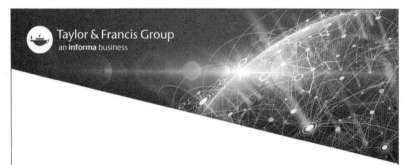